# By Faith They Went Out

## Occasional Papers, no. 20
## Institute of Mennonite Studies

Occasional Papers are occasional publications of the Institute of Mennonite Studies, the research agency of Associated Mennonite Biblical Seminary, Elkhart, Indiana. In the Occasional Papers series, IMS publishes essays in the fields of Bible, history, theology, and pastoral ministry, to foster discussion and to seek counsel, particularly from within the Mennonite theological community. Most essays are in finished form; some may be in a more germinal stage, released for purposes of testing and inviting critical response.

In accepting papers for publication, IMS gives priority to authors from the Council of Mennonite Seminaries (Associated Mennonite Biblical Seminary; Eastern Mennonite Seminary, Harrisonburg, Virginia; and Mennonite Brethren Biblical Seminary, Fresno, California); to faculty of Mennonite colleges; and to students and alumni of AMBS, EMS, and MBBS. Because Occasional Papers have limited circulation, authors are permitted to use their material in other scholarly settings, either for oral presentation or for publication.

# By
# Faith
# They
# Went
# Out

## Mennonite Missions
## 1850–1999

## Wilbert R. Shenk

Occasional Papers No. 20

Institute of Mennonite Studies
3003 Benham Avenue
Elkhart, Indiana 46517

2000

Institute of Mennonite Studies, 3003 Benham Avenue, Elkhart IN 46517-1999
© 2000 by Institute of Mennonite Studies

PRINTED IN THE UNITED STATES OF AMERICA

ISBN 0-936273-28-3


*Library of Congress Cataloging-in-Publication Data*

Shenk, Wilbert R.
   By faith they went out : Mennonite missions, 1850–1999 / Wilbert R. Shenk.
      p. cm. — (Occasional papers / Institute of Mennonite Studies ; no. 20)
Includes bibliographical references.
   ISBN 0-936273-28-3
   1. Mennonite Church—Missions—History—19th century. 2. Mennonite Church—Missions—History—20th century. I. Title. II. Occasional papers (Institute of Mennonite Studies (Elkhart, Ind.)) ; no. 20.
   BV2545 .S45 2000
   266'.97'09—dc21

                                          00-009797

# Contents

# *Preface*

This collection of essays makes Wilbert Shenk's dedicated and careful scholarship accessible to a wider audience. As such it is an important and timely contribution to the analysis of mission. This book is a welcome reminder that mission has the potential to provide focus and relevance to a church struggling for identity and meaning. Mission is God's gift to the church as well as to the world.

Shenk identifies the ongoing paradox between energetic Anabaptist missional roots and sluggish Mennonite missional reality. The missional energy and the unquestioned appeal of Anabaptist understandings of the faith seem incongruent with the missional ambivalence of Mennonite churches after they had survived the initial onslaught of persecution toward the end of the sixteenth century. Shenk suggests that this missional reluctance is the result of the severe persecution experienced by the church. This experience has led to two understandable trends in Mennonite churches. One is the trend toward assimilation with mainline Christendom churches, and the other is a trend toward isolation and silence. Both trends made the churches birthed by early Anabaptism reluctant to understand their role as active hosts inviting others to enter into their household of faith. Both trends also made these churches ambivalent about inviting others into a community whose self-image was one of having been misunderstood and victimized.

This ambivalence has continued to this day. Because of it, those in Mennonite/Brethren in Christ circles who have had a heart for mission have needed to look elsewhere for inspiration and guidance. Shenk repeatedly reminds the reader that Mennonite/Brethren in Christ mission theologies and strategies have been borrowed from Pietism, evangelicalism, fundamentalism, revivalism, the social gospel, and from ecumenical stimulation. The lack of self-generated missiology has led to coattail missiologies, attempts to do mission from Anabaptist perspectives using non-Anabaptist strategies.

The result has been that growth in Mennonite/Brethren in Christ churches has come in spite of ambivalence. Now the missiologically ambivalent church is challenged not only by borrowed theologies but also by new generations of Anabaptists all over the world who have not experienced ambivalence as part of their Anabaptist self-understandings. What the newer expressions of Anabaptist growth have in common with the ambivalence that birthed them is a dearth of serious missiological reflection. This lack in the newer churches is not now due to ambivalence toward the task but rather to what Shenk calls a Nike attitude: "Just do it." In either case, the rich contribution that Anabaptist experience and thinking could make to missiological reflection remains largely an untapped potential; it is again unavailable to the world.

Let me inject a personal note. I am not a trained missiologist. However, my biblical/theological training and my mission experience in Latin America confirm Shenk's observations about the ambivalence of my sending church and the aversion to reflection in the birthed churches. This is, however, changing at both ends. My church is genuinely seeking to overcome its ambivalence toward mission, and the Latin American churches are genuinely seeking to become more missiologically reflective. There is an enormous potential synergy if these two efforts can connect in a meaningful way, drawing on Anabaptist roots.

Shenk has some helpful suggestions about how to begin this mutually energizing process. One step is to encourage storytelling from each local perspective. Histories need to be written, not only institutional stories or "metropolitan" histories, but histories that hold "the local in its proper relationship with the global." This process, suggests Shenk, is critical to the survival of the church, "for the future of the church is inseparable from the mission dynamic. Where mission consciousness is extinguished, the church languishes and atrophies" (106–7). The global historiography project will help us understand the shift of the center of gravity from north to south.

A second step is to define much more carefully than we have what mission from an Anabaptist understanding would look like. According to Shenk, this project will require a will to move from maintenance to mission. He states: "The quest for recovery of the Anabaptist vision, which never realized its promise in the historical heartland of Europe and North America, lies in this direction. It will not be found in building more museums, holding more folk festivals, visiting more historical sites, and tracing more family genealogies. To recapture the Anabaptist vision we must above all else embrace a missionary consciousness" (118).

Shenk begins this process in chapter 6 by suggesting ten themes that he understands to be foundational for an Anabaptist missiology. These themes, he suggests, are common in the writings of many Anabaptist authors. They are a good beginning. But theological and historical restatement will not be enough to lift the Mennonite/Brethren in Christ churches in the north out of ambivalence and move them toward Anabaptist missional passion. We also need a profound conviction, based on personal and corporate experience, that life in Christ is better than life outside of Christ. If we prefer such a future in our own lives, we will be much more willing to commend it to others. Important as costly ethics, suffering service, and discipline may be, these elements must erupt in a personal and corporate sense of joy and a compelling vision of hope for a preferred future in Christ if we are to overcome our ambivalence and missional reluctance.

Fortunately, a profound sense of joy and a compelling vision of hope for a preferred future are exactly what characterize those churches in the south, birthed from missional ambivalence. We in the north wait to be converted.

*Robert J. Suderman, Executive Secretary*
*Ministries Commission, Mennonite Church Canada*

# Introduction

In 1947 the Dutch Mennonite Mission Association celebrated the centenary of its founding and what had been accomplished over the previous hundred years. The anniversary was overshadowed by the fact that World War 2 had ended only two years before, and the Netherlands was now embroiled in war with the Indonesians who were suing for their political independence. The present and the future were clouded by uncertainty. However, reviewing the results of the association's work from the beginning to 1947 put it all in a fresh perspective. One of the contributors to the anniversary booklet drew attention to the human tendency to despise "the day of small things" (Zech. 4:10). On the contrary, it is in and through these seemingly small and insignificant initiatives that God has accomplished the *missio Dei*. These are the experiences that build faith.

Although they trace their historical roots to 1525, Mennonites as an ecclesiastical group are relatively small. In 1850 their membership was confined to Europe and North America and numbered approximately 120,000 members. In the year 2000 total world membership of Mennonite and Brethren in Christ churches is approaching one million baptized members. In addition to growth in numbers, other changes have been taking place. The modern mission movement has been so preoccupied with carrying out the mandate to make disciples that it has scarcely recognized that the church that engages in mission will be changed by mission. One of the purposes of this book is to underscore the reflex action that mission has had on the sending churches in the West. We will also note evidence that the initiative in mission is being assumed by churches in Asia, Africa, and Latin America.

This is not an occasion for self-congratulation but for thanksgiving. The reasons for thanksgiving are multiple. In the first place, one must be grateful for those individuals of faith and faithfulness in the nineteenth century who broke rank with the status quo and drew Mennonites into missionary engagement. "By faith they went out" and many others followed. Second, one gives thanks for the substantially changed Mennonite identity, an identity that more fully reflects the diverse tongues and peoples of the world glimpsed at Pentecost and celebrated in the Parousia (Rev. 5). No one people group can adequately praise the God of the universe who created us all and desires the praise of all creation. The eschatological promise is that the choir of heaven will be representative of the whole of God's creation in offering up perpetual praise to our God and to the Lamb. A third reason for thanksgiving is the growing realization that our understanding of the work of Jesus Christ and his gospel is challenged, enlarged, and enriched as we see people in diverse places finding liberation and new life. The redeeming grace and power of God always exceed our expectations, but we discover this largely through the experiences of others with backgrounds dissimilar to our own. The fourth reason for thanksgiving is that, on the human level, our circle of friendships and fellowship has been greatly extended and enriched through the intercultural and international relationships formed during these 150 years.

The faith that motivated the Mennonite spiritual forebears remains a permanent challenge. The historical situation in the twenty-first century will be vastly different from that in 1850. We describe contemporary culture as postmodern; that is to say, an important shift is occurring and the worldview is no longer defined in terms of the pillars of modernity—rationality, the autonomous individual, science and technology—and the split between public and private, objective and subjective. And yet the sense of alienation and lack of hope that marks postmodern peoples has been manifestly present among all cultures down through the ages. How people hear the gospel is shaped by their cultural context, but the underlying spiritual need remains basically the same: to hear the good news that God in Jesus Christ has come to us—and continues to come to us—to offer us reconciliation with God and with our fellow human beings.

In 1955 I was assigned by the Mennonite Central Committee to work with the Mennonite Churches of Indonesia in north-central Java. Since then I have been concerned with the multiple dimensions of the Christian mission—as field worker, program administrator, student, teacher. I am convinced that today the church needs to be renewed and that that renewal will come if it is linked to the *missio Dei,* to God's missionary intention. Elsewhere I have worked out my theological vision of church and mission in terms of the mission dynamic.[1] The Mennonite experience in mission provides rich materials for studying the ways in

---

[1] Wilbert R. Shenk, *Changing Frontiers of Mission* (Maryknoll: Orbis Books, 1999), chap. 1.

which the mission dynamic has shaped this particular ecclesiastical tradition.

The essays presented here deal with several dimensions of the Mennonite experience in mission. For more than fifty years Mennonites have been stirred by the appeal to recover the Anabaptist vision. But a fundamental element of the Anabaptist inheritance has generally been overlooked. Therefore, I was pleased to be able to reflect on the theme of the Anabaptist roots of mission at the Bridgewater College Forum for Religious Studies in 1993. This paper was subsequently published in the volume, *Anabaptist Currents: History in Conversation with the Present*, edited by Carl F. Bowman and Stephen L. Longenecker (Bridgewater, Va.: Penobscot Press, 1995). I have revised this essay extensively for publication as chapter one here.

Chapter two is published here for the first time. Mennonites frequently display an ambivalent attitude toward the evangelical tradition. This may be due in part to an ignorance of the intertwining of evangelicalism and Mennonitism since the seventeenth century. The purpose of this chapter is to trace some of this interaction, especially as it relates to Mennonite mission history. The evangelical network has long been a matter of interest to me, but my interest was intensified when I began to notice some of the critical evangelical-Mennonite intersections that have had long-term implications.

In 1995 Mennonite Central Committee observed its seventy-fifth anniversary with several public events, including a symposium March 9–12, at Fresno, California. The paper I presented on that occasion was my effort to assess the way Mennonites have been changed by their involvement in mission and service during a historical period when the world has become increasingly bound together through transportation and communications technology. The paper was first published in *Mennonite Quarterly Review* 70 (January 1996), and has been revised for publication as chapter three of this volume.

Chapter four was written for the 1978 *Mennonite World Handbook*, edited by Paul N. Kraybill. It has been revised to bring the information up-to-date. I am grateful to Peter H. Rempel, executive secretary of the Council of International Ministries, for assistance in collecting the current data on which the revisions are based. This fresh information indicates that a new chapter in the Mennonite experience is beginning, based on the emergence of mission initiative outside Europe and North America.

Increasingly, we can describe Mennonite and Brethren in Christ reality in global terms. Indeed, we must do so if we are to grasp the significance of the changes of the past century and a half. At the same time, there is much work to be done to create the tools and materials to undergird the work of writing history and theology that engages this new reality. The fifth chapter was a paper presented at an international consultation of Mennonite and Brethren in Christ historians at Associated Mennonite Biblical Seminary in 1995, to explore the possibility of a coordinated effort at writing such a global history. The Global History Project under the aegis of Mennonite World Conference is providing follow-through. This paper was published in *Conrad Grebel Review* 15, no. 1/2 (winter/spring 1997), along with most of the other papers presented at the consultation. Minor changes have been made in what is published here.

For the past twenty-five years, a number of colleagues involved in Mennonite missions have been working toward a theology of mission that is biblical and that takes into account key convictions of the Anabaptist-Mennonite theological vision. I made a first attempt to draw together the main themes of these writings in one of the J. J. Thiessen Lectures at Canadian Mennonite Bible College in 1986. Subsequently, this paper was used for a consultation sponsored by the Council of International Ministries, and a portion of the present chapter six was included in the CIM compendium edited by Calvin E. Shenk, *A Relevant Anabaptist Missiology for the 1990s* (Council of International Ministries, 1990). I have revised it and present it here in full.

I am grateful to Willard M. Swartley, dean, Associated Mennonite Biblical Seminary, and Mary H. Schertz, director of the Institute of Mennonite Studies, for their encouragement and help in making this publication possible.

# List of Abbreviations

| | |
|---|---|
| AEM | Association of Evangelical Mennonite Churches of Brazil |
| AGM | Agape Gemeindewerk (Mennonitische Heimatmission) |
| AIMB | Association of Mennonite Churches of Brazil |
| AIMM | Africa Inter-Mennonite Mission (formerly Congo Inland Mission) |
| AMCCR | Association of Mennonites Churches of Costa Rica |
| Argentina | Argentine Mennonite Church |
| AV | Amor Viviente of Honduras |
| BIC | Brethren in Christ Board of Missions |
| Bielefeld MC | Mennonitengemeinde Bielefeld |
| BTG | Bund Taufgesinnter Gemeinden (Logos International) |
| CEM | Communauté Évangélique Mennonite du Congo |
| CGCM | Church of God in Christ, Mennonite |
| CIM | Congo Inland Mission (renamed Africa Inter-Mennonite Mission) |
| COM | Commission on Overseas Missions (formerly General Conference Mennonite Foreign Mission Board) |
| DMMA | Dutch Mennonite Mission Association |
| DMMK | Deutsches Mennonitisches Missionskomitee |
| EMB Paraguay | Evangelische Mennonitische Brudergemeinde, Paraguay |
| EMC (Can) | Evangelical Mennonite Conference of Canada Board of Missions |
| EMC (US) | Evangelical Mennonite Church Commission on Mission |
| EMEK | European Mennonite Evangelization Committee |
| EMM | Eastern Mennonite Missions (formerly Eastern Mennonite Board of Missions and Charities) |
| FMC | Franconia Mennonite Conference Mission Commission |
| FMMC | French Mennonite Missions Committee |
| GMC | Ghana Mennonite Church |
| JKI | Jemaat Kristen Indonesia/Indonesian Christian Churches |
| JMCC | Japan Mennonite Christian Church |
| KMB | Krimmer Mennonite Brethren |
| LI | Licht den Indianern |
| MB | Mennonite Brethren Board of Missions/Services |
| MBC/MCA | Mennonite Brethren in Christ/Missionary Church Association/ Missionary Church |
| MBM | Mennonite Board of Missions (formerly Mennonite Board of Missions and Charities) |
| MCC | Mennonite Central Committee |
| MK | Meserete Kristos (Ethiopian Mennonite Church) |
| PIPKA | Pengutusan Injil dan Pelayanan Kasih/Board of Missions and Service of Muria Christian Churches |
| PNMC | Pacific Northwest Mennonite Conference |
| RMM | Rosedale Mennonite Missions (formerly Conservative Mennonite Board of Missions/Charities) |
| SM | Community of Mennonite Congregations in Spain |
| SMM | Swiss Mennonite Mission |
| VMBMC | Virginia Mennonite Board of Missions and Charities |

# 1

## *Anabaptist Roots*

It was long accepted that mainstream church historians and theologians were either ignorant of the Anabaptist tradition or regarded it as of no importance in historical and theological studies of the period since the sixteenth century. This omission was substantially redressed in the twentieth century insofar as the Radical Reformation came to be accepted as one wing of the larger Reformation of the sixteenth century. Given the essentially nonmissionary ecclesiology that characterized the Reformation churches, it is perhaps not surprising that most scholars have turned a blind eye to the missionary character of the Anabaptist movement. Less understandable is the fact that after more than fifty years of research and writing on the missionary dimension of sixteenth-century Anabaptism—arguably one of the points of its greatest originality—the theme remains marginal to Anabaptist studies.[1]

---

Reprinted, with extensive revision, from Carl F. Bowman and Stephen L. Longenecker, eds., *Anabaptist Currents: History in Conversation with the Present* (Bridgewater, Va.: Penobscot Press, 1995), 289–302, by permission of the editors. © 1995 Forum for Religious Studies, Bridgewater College. Originally published as "Missions and Outreach: The Anabaptist Heritage."

[1] The two widely used works by Walter Klaassen, *Anabaptism: Neither Catholic nor Protestant* (Waterloo, Ont.: Conrad Press, 1973), and *Anabaptism in Outline: Selected Primary Sources* (Kitchener, Ont., and Scottdale, Pa.: Herald Press, 1981), contain no mention of the missionary dimension. John S. Oyer, "Historiography, Anabaptist," *The Mennonite Encyclopedia* (Scottdale, Pa., and Waterloo, Ont.: Herald Press, 1990), 5:378–82, though citing in his extensive bibliography several dissertations dealing with Anabaptist mission, omits reference to mission in his survey of the flowering of Anabaptist studies in the past forty years. J. Denny Weaver, *Becoming Anabaptist: The Origin and Significance of Sixteenth-Century Anabaptism* (Scottdale, Pa.: Herald Press, 1987), uses the term "mission" or "missionary" several times to describe the activity of certain sixteenth-century figures, but never suggests that an important dimension of the Anabaptist movement was its view of the church as a missionary presence in society. Weaver's work is valuable as a mirror of contemporary Mennonite self-understanding and the selective hanging on to the Anabaptist legacy. He suggests four regulative principles by which Anabaptist-Mennonites stake out their course in the modern world: separation,

Representative of the mainstream view is C. H. Robinson. In his *History of Christian Missions,* Robinson dates modern missions from the period 1580–1750.[2] After reviewing the attitudes of Luther, Zwingli, and Calvin with regard to missions, Robinson asserts that "the first theologian connected with the Reformation movements to maintain that 'the command to preach the gospel to all nations binds the Church' for all time was Adrianus Saravia."[3] In a 1590 treatise, Saravia called the church to follow in the train of the apostles by embracing the task of evangelizing the world.

Kenneth Scott Latourette, always scrupulous in his use of data and inclusive in scope, mentions the Anabaptists several times in volume three (covering the period 1500–1800) of his *History of the Expansion of Christianity.*[4] But what interests Latourette are the Anabaptist contributions to separation of church and state and gaining recognition for the rights of individual conscience. He takes no notice of the missionary character of sixteenth-century Anabaptism.

Gustav Warneck, pioneer of modern missiology, is unsparing in his critique of the attitude of the Reformers toward mission.[5] He identifies a number of reasons why the Reformers did not advocate missionary work. He candidly acknowledges that "we miss in the Reformers not only missionary action, but even the idea of missions, in the sense in which we understand them today."[6] Warneck brought to his study an

---

community, discipleship, nonresistance. This traditional Mennonite formulation is devoid of any compelling sense of mission to the world by which these regulative principles can be activated.

[2] Charles Henry Robinson, *History of Christian Missions* (Edinburgh: T. & T. Clark, 1915).

[3] Ibid., 43.

[4] Kenneth Scott Latourette, *Three Centuries of Advance; A.D. 1500–A.D. 1800,* vol. 3 of *A History of the Expansion of Christianity* (New York: Harper & Bros., 1939; reprint, Grand Rapids: Zondervan, 1970).

[5] For a thorough survey of the modern debate concerning the Reformers' attitudes toward mission, see the trenchant essay by John H. Yoder, "Reformation and Missions: A Literature Survey," in *Anabaptism and Mission,* ed. Wilbert R. Shenk (Scottdale, Pa., and Kitchener, Ont.: Herald Press, 1984), 40–50. Cf. David J. Bosch, *Transforming Mission: Paradigm Shifts in Theology of Mission* (Maryknoll: Orbis Books, 1991), 243–48.

[6] Gustav Warneck, *Outline of a History of Protestant Missions from the Reformation to the Present Time: A Contribution to Modern Church History,*

unshakeable commitment to maintaining the *corpus christianum*.[7] For him, mission was tied to territory. Mission must never be directed toward Christian lands. Christendom was obligated to. send missions to heathendom, and the term "mission" was reserved for this function alone, never as a way of describing the church's relation to its own environment. Warneck spoke of Christianization as the process of "filling the Volksatmosphere with Christian air." That is to say, Christianization is the means by which conditions are created for Volksconversion, which is the basis for the Volkskirche. Once this stage has been reached, the task of the church is to evangelize the people continually, to awaken them to their latent faith.[8]

In spite of the flowering of Anabaptist studies in the twentieth century and the increasing recognition that the sixteenth-century Anabaptists were a legitimate part of the Reformation, mission histories continued to pass over this chapter of history. This is especially odd in view of the substantial role played by the Free Churches in the modern mission movement.[9]

Eight decades after the death of Warneck in 1910, David J. Bosch, a leading figure in mission studies for the past thirty years, published his magnum opus, *Transforming Mission* (1991). In it he recognized the sixteenth-century Anabaptists as pioneers in the recovery of mission in

---

trans. George Robson (Edinburgh and London: Oliphant, Anderson and Ferrier, 1901), 9.

[7] In an address to the Centenary Missions Conference held in London in 1888, Warneck chided his Anglo-American colleagues: "Dear brethren in England and America, I believe that I speak in the name of all my German fellow-believers, if I urge upon you to cease from looking upon Germany, the land of Luther and Melanchthon, Arndt and Spener, Francke and Zinzendorf, Tholuck, Fliedner and Wichern, as a half heathen and rationalistic country." In James Johnston, ed., *Report of the Centenary Conference on Protestant Missions of the World* (London: James Nisbet and Co., 1888), 2:435. Warneck took umbrage at the fact that British Methodists were doing missionary work in Berlin.

[8] See Hans Kasdorf, *Gustav Warneck's missiologisches Erbe: Eine biographisch-historische Untersuchung* (Giessen: Brunnen Verlag, 1990), for a thorough study of Warneck's mission theory and theology.

[9] See my essay, "The 'Great Century' Reconsidered," in Shenk, *Anabaptism and Mission*, 158–77; and the rather cursory treatment by Kenneth Scott Latourette, "A People in the World: Historical Background," in James Leo Garrett, Jr., ed., *The Concept of the Believers' Church: Addresses from the 1967 Louisville Conference* (Scottdale, Pa.: Herald Press, 1969), 242–49.

the life of the (non–Roman Catholic) church precisely because of their alternative view of the nature of the church and their consequent rejection of territoriality.[10] The Anabaptists refused to cede absolute power to the state and the official church.[11] Only God was to be acknowledged as sovereign. Because they contested the absolutist claims of church and state, the Anabaptists were severely persecuted by both.

A clarifying note is called for at this point. In discussions of the relationship of church and society, the Anabaptist model continues to be cited as the one that calls for the strict separation of the church from society, and withdrawal from social responsibility by Christians. The Anabaptist Schleitheim Confession or Schleitheim Brotherly Union of 1527, with its teaching on the oath and sword, is cited as the basis for this "sectarian" response.[12] Two points need to be made. (1) Rejecting both the *corpus christianum* and the Protestant Reformation's response to it, the Anabaptists had to find a compelling basis for their critique. Early Anabaptist teaching and documents such as the Schleitheim Confession provided the rationale for separation of the powers, thus breaking the absolute power of state and church. The authority of both was relativized. The history of the next sixty or seventy years demonstrates that the Anabaptists were anything but disengaged. Indeed, their continuing critique of the socioreligious and political status quo resulted in severe and certain response from both church and state. (2) The Mennonite descendents of the Anabaptists, with the exception of the Dutch, did withdraw from societal involvement. They were confronted with a difficult tactical choice: *(a)* continue to press their critique of church and state, an alternative that entailed the likelihood of extermination, or *(b)* form religious enclaves where they could maintain

---

[10] Bosch, *Transforming Mission,* 245–47.

[11] In his essay, "Anabaptist Missions and the Critique of Christendom," John D. Roth summarizes the "essential features of Christendom: a church with universal and exclusive spiritual authority, woven into the cultural fabric of medieval society and welded firmly to the political interests of feudal lords and the early modern state." In David W. Shenk and Linford Stutzman, eds., *Practicing Truth: Confident Witness in Our Pluralistic World* (Scottdale, Pa.: Herald Press, 1999), 85.

[12] Ernst Troeltsch, *The Social Teaching of the Christian Churches* (New York: Harper, 1960) has an extensive discussion of "church" and "sect" (e.g., 691–729). Unfortunately, a reductionist reading of Troeltsch has led to a simplistic use of his typology.

their religious convictions and way of life. For choosing the latter they have been endlessly criticized by the Christian mainstream. But the point to be made here is that the Mennonite "sin" of withdrawal should not be incorrectly charged to the Anabaptist account.[13]

## ANABAPTIST MISSIONARY ACTIVITY

All references to "Anabaptist" and "Anabaptist mission" in this chapter have to do with the period 1525–ca.1590. The remnant thereafter is identified as Mennonites, Hutterites, and Brethren. By the end of the sixteenth century these erstwhile Anabaptists had deeply sublimated the missionary dynamic and a new ethos had emerged.

The most comprehensive study of Anabaptist missionary outreach to date is that by Wolfgang Schäufele, *Das missionarische Bewußtsein und Wirken der Täufer* (1966).[14] Other studies have concentrated on particular aspects of Anabaptist mission: mission impulse, the use of Scripture, and the view of church. In addition, there are numerous scattered references to individual Anabaptists engaged in outreach, which provide further clues to the scope of their witness.

### Zollikon

The final step in the rupture between the Zurich Reformer Huldreich Zwingli and the nascent Anabaptist group was the baptism the evening of January 21, 1525, of Conrad Grebel, Felix Manz, George Blaurock and others. The authorities acted swiftly to suppress this new movement by banishing or imprisoning those involved. The locus of activity quickly shifted to nearby Zollikon. It was here that in the days following, the premier Anabaptist congregation was formed among farmers and artisans.[15]

Two Christian rites had come to symbolize the disagreement between Zwingli and the rebel group: baptism and the Lord's Supper.

---

[13] H. Richard Niebuhr, *Christ and Culture* (New York: Harper, 1956), states: "The Mennonites have come to represent the attitude [of living under the Lordship of Christ alone] most purely, since they not only renounce all participation in politics and refuse to be drawn into military service..." (56). Niebuhr uses Mennonites as representative of his "Christ against culture" type.

[14] Wolfgang Schäufele, *Das missionarische Bewußtsein und Wirken der Täufer* (Neukirchen-Vluyn: Neukirchener Verlag, 1966).

[15] Fritz Blanke, *Brothers in Christ,* trans. Joseph Nordenhaug (Scottdale, Pa.: Herald Press, 1961), traces and analyzes these developments.

The Anabaptists called for reform of both the theology of these rites and their ceremonial observance. The house fellowship now meeting in Zollikon considered itself fully church and unhesitatingly administered baptism on confession of faith, and observed the Lord's Supper with lay people breaking ordinary bread and serving the cup to all participants. This marks the birth of the Believers/Free Church within the Reformation in 1525.

In addition to challenging the regnant meaning of baptism and the Lord's Supper, the Anabaptists redefined the church to mean those who had repented and experienced conversion and voluntarily accepted baptism. This crisis experience issued in a deepened sense of personal responsibility.

Although the Zollikon Anabaptist congregation itself did not last long under efficient official repression, its evangelizing initiatives spread rapidly to the surrounding areas. Much of this witness was given by inconspicuous personal contact. Since the movement remained largely a cell-group or house church, many people were brought to faith in these fellowships. Thus, each congregation was a center for evangelization and every member was directly related to the action.[16]

Zollikon also began sending missioners. Marx Bosshard, a young Zollikon farmer, was baptized in the early days of the Anabaptist movement. Later in 1525 Bosshard was serving as an itinerant Anabaptist preacher in the highlands of Zurich.[17] For this he had several

---

[16] The "discovery" in the twentieth century of the importance of the laity for the mission of the church is noteworthy. This has taken two forms. (1) The theological reformulation is represented by a spate of books, starting in the 1950s with French Catholic theologian Yves Congar's *Lay People in the Church*, trans. Donald Attwater (Westminster, Md.: Newman Press, 1957); originally published as *Jalons pour une théologie du laïcat* (Paris: Éditions du Cerf, 1953); and Hendrik Kraemer's *A Theology of the Laity* (Philadelphia: Westminster, 1958). (2) In terms of mission theory, the best-known experiment has been Evangelism-in-Depth, pioneered by R. Kenneth Strachan, leader of the Latin America Mission, who around 1960 propounded the theorem: "The expansion of any movement is in direct proportion to its success in mobilizing its total membership in continuous propagation of its beliefs" (Strachan, *The Inescapable Calling* [Grand Rapids: Wm. B. Eerdmans Co., 1968], 108). Strachan's starting point was his concern for renewal of the church in Latin America, and he formulated his theorem in response. Later he recognized its rootage in the reality of the primitive church.

[17] Blanke, *Brothers in Christ*, 28.

role models, including George Blaurock, known for his fiery preaching and wide itineracy.

Essentially, the Anabaptist movement spread through two complementary actions, both characteristic of the New Testament church. On the one hand, leaders with apostolic gifts traveled far and wide preaching, baptizing, and organizing new congregations. On the other hand, members of each congregation were actively engaged in witness in their community and region in the course of daily living. What we have already observed of the Zollikon congregation became a widespread pattern among Anabaptist congregations.

*Apostolic Leaders*

Hans Hut has been called the apostle of the Anabaptists in Upper Austria. Herbert Klassen concluded: "If the contribution of Hans Hut's life lies in the fact that he baptized more converts, founded more new congregations and commissioned more Anabaptist apostles than any other early leader in South Germany, then the contribution of his teaching lies in his clear delineation of the crucial role of suffering discipleship, and the corporate nature and missionary character of the church-brotherhood."[18] Hut's ministry lasted only sixteen months. Following his baptism on May 26, 1526, at Augsburg, Hut went to Haina where he won a number of converts; then he went to Erlangen. Next he went to Swabia and thence to Austria and Moravia. He returned to Augsburg and from there went to Nicolsburg at the end of 1526. In 1527 Hut traveled to Vienna, Melk, and Steyr. Escaping arrest there, he fled to Freistadt, Upper Austria. He next visited Gallneukirchen and Linz, "preaching and baptizing everywhere."[19] He had also worked at Passau, Schärding, Braunau, Lauren, and Salzburg. By August 1527 Hut was back in Augsburg for the special conference. In September he was

---

[18] Herbert Klassen, "The Life and Teaching of Hans Hut," *Mennonite Quarterly Review* 33 (July 1959): 205. The more recent scholarly debate over the Hut legacy is not of immediate concern. Our interest is only descriptive, with reference to the role he played as leader of the Anabaptist movement in Austria and South Germany in its formative stage. See Ray C. Gingerich, *The Mission Impulse of Early Swiss and South German–Austrian Anabaptists* (Ph.D. diss., Vanderbilt University, 1980), for a sorting out of the issues around Hut's theology and relationships.

[19] "Hut, Hans," *The Mennonite Encyclopedia* (Scottdale, Pa.: Mennonite Publishing House; Newton, Kans.: Mennonite Publication Office; Hillsboro, Kans.: Mennonite Brethren Publishing House, 1956), 2:848.

arrested and died December 6, 1527, while awaiting trial. Wherever Hut went, he evangelized, baptized, admonished, and assisted the local congregations. It is apparent that Anabaptist believers were already present in many of the places he visited. This means that the movement had spread rapidly in the fifteen months after January 1525.

The outstanding Anabaptist apostle of the second generation was the Dutch elder Leenaert Bouwens (1515–1582). During the thirty years 1551–82 Bouwens ranged as far north as Holstein, North Germany; south to France; and east to Poland. He kept records of his journeys and of the number of people he baptized. His ministry fell into five discrete periods: 1551–54 (869 baptisms), 1554–56 (693 baptisms), 1557–61 (808 baptisms), 1563–65 (4,499 baptisms), and 1568–82 (3,509 baptisms), for a reported total of 10,378 people baptized.[20]

Hut and Bouwens are representative of Anabaptist apostles who itinerated widely and did much both to spread the message as well as to stabilize and build up the local congregations throughout northern and central Europe.

*Anabaptist Laity*

Though we have already made the point that the rank and file played a full role in the spread of the Anabaptist movement, it is necessary to examine this further.[21] People who decided to become Anabaptists knew from the outset that in spite of the likelihood of persecution, they would assume responsibility to witness to their faith in the world. This was accepted positively as a privilege rather than as a legal requirement. It was understood that these lay members were called to evangelize and

---

[20] "Leenaert Bouwens," *The Mennonite Encyclopedia* (Scottdale, Pa.: Mennonite Publishing House; Newton, Kans.: Mennonite Publication Office; Hillsboro, Kans.: Mennonite Brethren Publishing House, 1957), 3:305; and N. van der Zijpp, "From Anabaptist Congregation to Mennonite Seclusion," in Shenk, *Anabaptism and Mission*, 121.

[21] This section follows Wolfgang Schäufele, "The Missionary Vision and Activity of the Anabaptist Laity," in Shenk, *Anabaptism and Mission*, 70–87. (This essay summarizes Schäufele's dissertation, *Das missionarische Bewußtsein und Wirken der Täufer*.) Schäufele shows that this early emphasis on lay responsibility and participation soon began to be damped by the growing role of ordained leaders in baptizing and organizing congregations. A practical reason for this was that (re)baptizing was a crime. If it was done by an itinerant evangelist, most of whom were ordained, there was less likelihood of arrest than if it was carried out by local residents.

invite people to repent, but baptism was administered by ordained leaders.

From testimony preserved in court records one gets a clear impression of the sincerity, conviction, and zeal that motivated these lay members. A peasant, Hans von Rüblingen, at his trial in Passau in 1535 insisted that he and his cohorts compelled no one to join them, "but wherever they traveled or lived they spoke the word of the Lord."[22]

Anabaptist lay members used natural lines of relationship as channels of witness to family members, neighbors, friends, occupational colleagues, and employers. A Tyrolean master shoemaker, Valtein Luckner, had as apprentice Matheis, an Anabaptist, who engaged his master in conversation about the Bible and matters of faith. Later at his own trial, Luckner relied on the statement of Matheis in summarizing his convictions: "One must live according to the will of God and be baptized according to faith."[23] He had been baptized by Jacob Hutter in 1530.

Based on his extensive study of Anabaptist missionary activity in South Germany, Schäufele concludes that "the woman in Anabaptism emerges as a fully emancipated person in religious matters and as the independent bearer of Christian convictions."[24] Many accounts show women to have been vigorous evangelists among their families and friends, and in their communities. Late in the sixteenth century, the Württemberg government still considered Anabaptist women to be a serious threat because they "spread their faith through word of mouth or through booklets."[25] The government ordered single women to be expelled from the province and married women to be chained at home.

It was widely acknowledged that what gave particular power to the testimony of these Anabaptists was their exemplary lifestyle. In a period noted for low morals, the Anabaptists sought to put the ethical principles of the gospel into practice in daily discipleship. This did not save them from continuous persecution; rather they tried to maintain a clear conscience in a hostile world.

---

[22] Ibid., 73.

[23] Ibid., 77.

[24] Ibid., 79. Over time the role of women, and of the laity in general, was increasingly circumscribed. Further research is needed to clarify this and related questions.

[25] Ibid., 80.

## Mission Strategy

From what has been said thus far it might be inferred that Anabaptist missions were largely unorganized and uncoordinated. In one respect this is undoubtedly true. Certainly, the local lay witness through hundreds of congregations proceeded essentially on this basis. But this is not the whole story.

In August 1527 a group of more than sixty Anabaptist leaders met in Augsburg.[26] In contrast to the Schleitheim meeting held earlier that year, the Augsburg conclave produced no written documents. From contemporary accounts, however, it appears that several actions were taken. Most significant, the conference gave attention to the need for a comprehensive plan for evangelizing Europe. The conference authorized missionary teams that went out from the meeting in small groups to visit existing Anabaptist congregations for the purpose of strengthening these groups as well as establishing new congregations.

This concerted witness caused a further expansion of the movement with the inevitable result that civil and ecclesiastical authorities quickly took action against them. Within a year nearly all of these missioners had been martyred; this meeting has come to be known as the Martyrs' Synod. This was only the first stage in formal planning for missionary action by Anabaptists.

## Mission Methods

The methods employed by the Anabaptists were basic: person-to-person witness and preaching to groups. However, virtually all of the preaching undertaken by the Anabaptists was considered illegal because it was being done by people not recognized as clergy by either the Roman Catholic or Protestant churches and in places not consecrated for religious services. Wilhelm Wiswedel has described how they went about holding meetings:

---

[26] "Martyrs' Synod," *Mennonite Encyclopedia,* 3:529–31. Scholars disagree about the nature of the Augsburg meeting, i.e., was it was to deal with Hans Hut's apocalyptic teachings, or with developing an evangelistic strategy? Schäufele, *Das missionarische Bewußtsein,* 148–53, gives a convincing account from the latter viewpoint. For a reconstruction of the event and evaluation of its significance, see Gingerich, *Mission Impulse,* 305–21. Gingerich summarizes the Augsburg program that undergirds the mission impulse as including: active engagement, covenantal community, eschatological expectation, persecution, collaboration of religio-political establishment against the Anabaptists, and eschatological "pull from beyond."

Usually they had their gatherings in a forest. In the Forest of Strassburg, for example, they had as many as 300 people in one single meeting. They also met regularly in the Ringlinger Forest at Bretten, in the Schillingswald between Olbronn and Knittlingen, and in the Forest of Prussia near Aachen. These meetings were held between 10:00 p.m. and 2:00 a.m. In the section of the forest called *Bregehren* at Walkerbach in Wuerttemberg one can still find a pulpit-like rock known as *Gaisstein* where they conducted their worship and gospel services with the aid of two lanterns to dispel the darkness. In addition, they met in isolated mills, such as the one at Kleinleutersdorf in Orlammunde, or at the sawmill in Zorge on the Harz and in similar places. Peter Valk preached in a sheep barn at Saal in Thuringia. Enders Feckelein preached to a number of people sitting there with open Bibles around two tables in a blacksmith shop. Sometimes they gathered for meetings at places that would allow them to escape quickly from the hands of persecutors in the event they were found out. In Tirol, for example, they met on remote farms, in sand pits, and in the shelters of huge rocks. But not all places were hideouts. There were at least two castles where the Anabaptist missionaries evangelized. One was the Schloss Munichau at Kitzbuhl and the other the Schloss Neuhof at Brunneck in Tirol. The records also show that these meetings generally drew large crowds.[27]

In such circumstances there is no scope for sophisticated methods and experimentation. Combining courage and cunning these Anabaptists persisted in sharing their faith with many eager inquirers using the most rudimentary means available to them.

## Hutterian Missions

Of all Anabaptists, the Hutterites had the most developed mission approach and continued this work longer than any other group.[28] Without this continuous missionary action they would never have won thousands of new members to their communitarian way of life. The Hutterites sent out missioners each spring and autumn. Over the years they covered the

---

[27] Cited by Hans Kasdorf, "The Anabaptist Approach to Mission," in Shenk, *Anabaptism and Mission*, 54–55.

[28] These paragraphs follow Leonard Gross, *The Golden Years of the Hutterites: The Witness and Thought of the Communal Moravian Anabaptists during the Walpot Era, 1565–1578* (Scottdale, Pa.: Herald Press, 1980), chapter 3; and Leonard Gross, "Sixteenth Century Hutterian Mission," in Shenk, *Anabaptism and Mission*, 97–118.

whole of Germany and Austria, as well as visiting Switzerland, Italy, Belgium, the Netherlands, Poland, Bohemia, Slovakia, and Denmark. Such an effort could only be sustained by careful planning, preparation, and implementation. They kept records of their journeys and reported results.

The Hutterites developed a formal training program. Whether the school trained only those going out on mission assignments or was intended as a kind of basic formation in Christian discipleship for all new members is unclear.[29] The curriculum was organized under three rubrics: (1) biblical history as warning, (2) penitential preaching *(Bußpredigt)* about how bad the world is, and (3) teaching concerning the church. Under the last head seventeen topics were covered, including the need for forgiveness of sin, growing in faith and becoming mature in Christ, life in the Spirit, the meaning of the gospel, the mission task, relationship to the world, an extended section on Christian community, baptism and the Lord's Supper, and Christian character (including *Gelassenheit* [yieldedness] and *Gehorsam* [obedience]). This training was practical and foundational.

Other resources were also provided to Hutterite missioners. A tract, "Valuable Directions and Instructions on How to Turn Unbelievers from Their Error,"[30] assumed to have been written by Leonhard Dax in the 1560s, was composed especially for missionary use. The tract discusses the human condition and need for God, the nature of the Christian community, and relationship to the world that does not recognize God. It then urges people to come to faith in Jesus Christ and join the body of Christ.

A MISSIONARY ECCLESIOLOGY

As noted at the beginning of this chapter, Christendom ecclesiology was geared to a situation in which the whole society was said to be Christian. By definition, missionary witness was excluded. When mission was contemplated, it was left to religious orders dedicated to working beyond the bounds of "Christian" lands. The Radical Reformers challenged precisely this formulation by taking issue with the official ecclesiology.

---

[29] Wilhelm Wiswedel, "Die alten Täufergemeinden und ihr missionarisches Wirken," *Archiv für Reformationsgeschichte* 41 (1948): 115. Wiswedel bases his description on the Codex Ritualis of 1590.

[30] Gross, *Golden Years*, 46.

## The Great Commission

The Reformation of the sixteenth century had to do with the nature of the church. The Anabaptists envisioned a restored New Testament church. A variety of formulations have been put forward as to what this meant in the sixteenth century and how it was to be achieved. One such interpretive framework is based on the premise that Anabaptism was a missionary movement for which the charter was the Great Commission.

In 1946 Franklin H. Littell wrote a pioneering essay, "The Anabaptist Theology of Mission," in which he asserts: "No words of the Master were given more serious attention by his Anabaptist followers than his final command."[31] This observation has been echoed by others in the years since. Heinold Fast says "A glance of the *Täuferakte[n]*, which have an index of Scripture references, shows that this was the most quoted Scripture passage among the Anabaptists. With this passage infant baptism could be renounced easily and clearly, and the legitimacy of baptism by faith demonstrated."[32] This established the irrefutable basis for evangelization in the world.

But this interpretation has been challenged. Ray C. Gingerich insists, "We must reject, on the basis of the historical evidence, Littell's thesis regarding the centrality of the Great Commission in the mission consciousness of the Swiss and the South German–Austrian Anabaptists."[33] According to Gingerich the Great Commission did not figure in the 1527 Augsburg conference and is not "the key to an understanding of the Anabaptist mission" generally. Critics believe the source of Anabaptist mission to lie deep in the nature of the church as the community that incarnates the life of Jesus as expressed in the socioreligious reality of the Anabaptist movement itself.

---

[31] Shenk, *Anabaptism and Mission*, 18; and Franklin Hamlin Littell, "The Great Commission," chap. 4 in *The Origins of Sectarian Protestantism: A Study of the Anabaptist View of the Church* (New York: Macmillan, 1964), which contains various parallel statements.

[32] Heinold Fast, "The Anabaptist Understanding of Jesus' Great Commission," *Mission Focus* 11 (March 1983): 4–5.

[33] Gingerich, *Mission Impulse,* 335. It must be kept in mind that Gingerich bases his analysis on the model from the sociological theory of Peter L. Berger and Thomas Luckmann. This model has its own inherent limitations. See note 22 for a summary of defining influences of the Anabaptist mission impulse. For Gingerich's analysis the key Scripture is Matthew 18:15–20 (Gingerich, *Mission Impulse,* 36–37).

At issue here is not whether the Anabaptists acted in missionary ways by seeking to evangelize widely in Europe. Rather the question centers on the source of motivation and on the Anabaptists' conceptualization of what they were doing.

It is beyond the scope of the present essay to explore this debate thoroughly. Several summary comments must serve as a bridge to the next section. First, even a cursory reading of the sources shows that the Anabaptists—from as early as Manz's 1524 "Protestation"—consistently used particularly the Matthean and Markan versions of the Great Commission as the basis for their attack on pedobaptism and for their advocacy of believers baptism. Sometimes, but not always, they linked this to the preaching of the gospel. Second, Littell and others who have emphasized the central role of the Great Commission have also recognized the way it was used as the basis for teaching believers baptism. Third, we need to ask how the Great Commission was used by the second generation leaders such as Menno Simons and the Hutterians. Did they continue to find both believers baptism and mission in the Great Commission? In his "Reply to Gellius Faber," Menno said: "Yet through no other command nor ordinance than to preach the Gospel, make disciples by means of the doctrine, baptize these same disciples, and so gather unto the Lord a peculiar people, who should walk in Christ Jesus in righteousness, truth, and obedience, as the regenerate children of God..."[34] This statement points to continuity between Manz and others of the first generation and Menno of the second.

## The Great Commission in Recent Scholarship

One of the criticisms made both by those who believe the Great Commission played a role in defining the missionary dimension of Anabaptism and by those who reject this interpretation is that we are reading twentieth-century assumptions and questions back into the sixteenth century. In other words, the Great Commission has become stereotyped as the so-called charter of the modern missionary movement and we misuse it when we try to understand a sixteenth-century movement through this frame. Thus, at one point Gingerich dismisses

---

[34] John Christian Wenger, ed., and Leonard Verduin, trans., *The Complete Writings of Menno Simons* (Scottdale, Pa.: Herald Press, 1956), 701. See also pp. 120, 303, 394, 633, 676, 681–82, 739. Menno moves easily between the baptism and evangelizing/discipling themes but generally keeps them integrally related.

Littell's argument, saying, "Our study so far indicates that the passage was given ecclesiological significance, not mission except by implication."[35] Here the debate is made to turn on whether the Great Commission has ecclesiological or missiological meaning.

New Testament exegetes have done fresh work in recent years on the interpretation of the Great Commission that points to an alternative interpretation. The main lines of argument are as follows.

In the first place, it is a mistake to treat the Great Commission as an appendage to or separable from the rest of the Gospels.[36] Essentially, this was what the Reformers did when they argued that these words, having been fulfilled by the first apostles, were no longer binding on the church. On the contrary, the Great Commission brings the development within each of the Gospels to a climax. One cannot fully grasp what has preceded if the climax is detached.

This leads to the second point. The Great Commission is the key ecclesiological statement in the Gospels, so ecclesiology must always be interpreted missionally and mission must be interpreted ecclesially.[37] Thus the Great Commission, freed from historical accretions and captivity to a slogan status, has the potential to challenge the ever-present centripetal tendency of the institutional church to focus in on itself.

Third, viewed in this light, the Great Commission ought to be the basis for structuring or institutionalizing the church's relation to the world. The Great Commission calls us to understand the nature and work

---

[35] Gingerich, *Mission Impulse,* 83, n.224.

[36] See Bosch, *Transforming Mission,* 56–57; Lucien Legrand, "The Missionary Command of the Risen Christ," *Indian Theological Studies* 23, no. 3 (September 1986): 302–7; and Otto Michel, "The Conclusion of Matthew's Gospel: A Contribution to the History of the Easter Message," in *The Interpretation of Matthew,* ed. Graham Stanton (Philadelphia: Fortress Press, 1983), 35.

[37] Gingerich, *Mission Impulse*, 29, speaks movingly of the importance of mission to the ongoing vitality of the church: "Ultimately the movement turned back upon its own participants, ever anew infusing them with the power that impelled them as missioners. Those who sought to be redeeming, were the recipients of the redemption they proclaimed. The saving missioners, as they perceived it, became the saved ones. This dialectic between...the Movement and the individual participants, was reflected in the motif of eschatological participatory solidarity with Christ." It is inadequate to take Matthew 18:15–20, with its inward focus on church order, as the basis for a doctrine of the church. Matthew 18:15–20 must be seen within the overall development of the messianic movement that Jesus instigates.

of the church in terms of its mission to be the body of Jesus the Messiah in the world, thereby continuing and extending his reconciling work in this eschatological age.

*The Church-World Nexus*

This brings us to the heart of the matter. We cannot turn to the sixteenth-century Anabaptists for an exposition of a theology of mission as that has been developed in the twentieth century. (One should bear in mind that such systematic theological writing on mission has made its appearance only since 1945. And much of it remains in the shadow of the Christendom view of mission.) But we may argue with confidence that the early Anabaptists, relying on their biblicist approach to Scripture and reading their sociopolitical times in light of the eschaton, were on firm ground in their interpretation of the church's relationship to the world. Intuitively they found in the Great Commission the power both to challenge the *corpus christianum*—in their rejection of pedobaptism and all that this symbolized—and to form themselves into local communities of faith that assumed responsibility for evangelizing the world. Anabaptists thus negated the principle of territoriality. Their commitment was to live out the reality of the Messiah's eschatological reign. The consciousness of being called into service by the Messiah on behalf of the new order of salvation inevitably placed them at odds with the old order in which they believed the majority churches to be deeply embedded. Withdrawal from society was not an option for the Anabaptists. The only faithful response was that of missionary witness regardless of the cost. The inevitable and logical consequence was that the Anabaptists should be a church of martyrs.[38]

## A CONTEXTUAL GOSPEL

When a movement evokes the kind of response that met the Anabaptists, it is because the message they conveyed found deep resonance.[39]

---

[38] The remarkable essay by Ethelbert Stauffer, "The Anabaptist Theology of Martyrdom," *Mennonite Quarterly Review* 19 (1945): 179–214, focuses the issue sharply.

[39] Harold S. Bender, "The Anabaptist Vision," in Guy F. Hershberger, *The Recovery of the Anabaptist Vision* (Scottdale, Pa.: Herald Press, 1957), 31, quotes Sebastian Franck, an opponent of the Anabaptists writing in 1531: "The Anabaptists spread so rapidly that their teaching soon covered the land as it were. They soon gained a large following, and baptized thousands, drawing to themselves many sincere souls who had a zeal for God."

Undoubtedly, some of the Anabaptist evangelists and missionaries were outstanding communicators, but the rapid progress of the movement across Europe in such a short time cannot be accounted for in terms of the number of effective preachers. It was a people movement that depended greatly on a network of lay people. The Anabaptist message spread not simply because of eloquent and effective preaching but because it was a highly contextual message. That is, the Anabaptist message addressed the situation of the people of Europe at that time and offered a diagnosis of the ills of church and society, proposed a compelling alternative, and conveyed a sense of hope. This is evidence of an effectively contextualized message. It can be analyzed in terms of the triad: world, word, church.

## World

By the sixteenth century the *corpus christianum* was more than a millennium old. The Constantinian synthesis of church and state had become corrupt, and criticism was widespread. Attempts at reform of the church such as that of Jan Hus (ca. 1372–1415) had been made repeatedly throughout the centuries. The Catholic Church reacted decisively to extirpate all opposition. The essence of Constantinianism was coercion. It was a system maintained by the sword. By the sixteenth century resentment against the church had intensified and the desire for change was widespread. This unrest produced the oxygen that enabled Martin Luther and the other Reformers to succeed in breaking the grip of the Catholic Church in western Europe.[40] Not all agreed that the Protestant Reformers had gone far enough. In the aftermath of Reformation, the Protestant church replaced the Catholic Church as the religion of state. The underlying issue of oppressive and unjust government was brushed aside by both Catholics and Protestants.[41] The

---

[40] In effect the Catholic Church did eventually acknowledge the legitimacy of the criticisms in convening the Council of Trent, 1545–1551. One of the key reforms instituted by Trent was more adequate training for priests and new standards of pastoral care and supervision of priests.

[41] Cf. Harold S. Bender, *The Anabaptists and Religious Liberty in the Sixteenth Century* (Philadelphia: Fortress Press, 1970), who argues that neither Catholics nor Protestants promoted religious liberty in the sixteenth century. The Anabaptist argument in favor of religious liberty gained ground only later. Eventually it became the ideal underlying separation of church and state. Paul P. Peachey, "The Radical Reformation, Political Pluralism, and the Corpus Christianum," in *The Origins and Characteristics of Anabaptism: Proceedings*

Anabaptists refused to settle for so-called reform. They regarded the Reformation as a sham and a palliative because it failed to address the root problems of church and society. Instead of fulfilling its God-ordained role to be protector of the people, the government, with the blessing and support of the church, was the leading oppressor. Menno Simons lived a fugitive existence almost continuously after he embraced the Anabaptist message in 1536. He worked tirelessly to mitigate the civil sanctions imposed by church and state against religious dissenters, appealing to the magistracy: "With proper pity be at least somewhat concerned about the inhuman and heavy oppression, misery, distress, cross, and torture of your sad and innocent subjects."[42] In their preaching and writing, Anabaptists constantly addressed the socioeconomic plight of the masses. On the one hand, they offered encouragement and comfort to the people and, on the other, they confronted the authorities for their failure to govern justly for they, too, were under God's authority.

*Word*

The starting point for the Anabaptist message was Scripture. According to Menno Simons, the Word is the "seed...whereby we are begotten of God...like unto [God's] image, nature, and being."[43] The central Anabaptist concern was that people be led to genuine repentance from sin and spiritual regeneration that produced authentic Christian discipleship. Only the Word of God contained the seed of renewal or regeneration. It is the Word alone that "changes and renews the whole man, that is, from the carnal to the spiritual, the earthly to the spiritual; it transforms from death unto life, from unbelief to belief.... For through this seed all nations upon the earth are blessed."[44] This message was addressed to people in a context in which religion was defined by form and ritual. Salvation was mediated through the rites of the church and dispensed by the clergy. But this religious system had failed to produce the fruits of true godliness. It did not touch the core issues of life. Many

---

*of the Colloquium Organized by the Faculty of Protestant Theology of Strasbourg, 20–22 Feb 1975*, ed. Marc Lienhard (The Hague: M. Nijhoff, 1977), 10–26, emphasizes that the initial Anabaptist impulse was to advocate a pluralist vision that respected individual conscience.

[42] Wenger, *Menno Simons,* 117.

[43] Ibid., 57.

[44] Ibid.

people had lost respect for the system and were desperate for an alternative. They wanted a vital personal relationship with God.

Menno Simons insisted that true faith would result in ethical fruit. He warned against the claim "that faith alone saves, without any assistance by works." He held that this kind of teaching misleads people into thinking that how they live is of no consequence; rather it gives "free rein" and encourages unrighteous living.[45] "The true evangelical faith which makes the heart upright and pious before God, moves, changes, urges, and constrains a man so that he will always hate the evil and gladly do the things which are right and good."[46] The Word is indeed the only seed that produces fruit that is pleasing to God.

## *Church*

The Anabaptist message addressed the question of the church from two angles. Anabaptists continually inveighed against what they regarded as a corrupt church that dishonored its head, Jesus Christ, by its failures.[47] At the same time the Anabaptists called for the restoration of the church as Christ had intended it to be, the worthy bride of Christ. This would be a body composed of regenerated individuals who had voluntarily become members of Christ's body, the church.[48] Such a church would be identified by six marks: (1) an unadulterated, pure doctrine, (2) a scriptural use of sacramental signs, (3) obedience to the Word, (4) unfeigned brotherly love, (5) a bold confession of God and Jesus Christ, and (6) oppression and tribulation for the sake of the Lord's Word.[49] Anabaptists judged the Protestant Reformation to be a failure. They insisted on restitution of the primitive ecclesial ideal rather than the reformation of a corrupt ecclesial body. Only a return to the apostolic standard would result in the kind of church Jesus had intended his body to be. The masses that felt oppressed as much by church as by state—for the church acted as agent of the state in official matters—heard this vision of the church as an authentic alternative, one that offered hope.

---

[45] Ibid., 333.

[46] Ibid., 337.

[47] Cf. Bender, "Anabaptist Vision," 40–42.

[48] Bender, "Anabaptist Vision," gives this as the second of three defining characteristics of the Anabaptist vision.

[49] C. J. Dyck, "The Anabaptist Understanding of the Good News," in Shenk, *Anabaptism and Mission,* 36. These marks are drawn from the writings of Menno Simons.

The kind of church implicit in these six defining characteristics stood out in bold relief against the background of the existing church. It had the ring of authenticity about it. Notwithstanding the persistence of official persecution, thousands chose to be a part of this kind of church.

CONCLUSION

The vision of the church that is at the heart of the Anabaptist movement in the sixteenth century may be summarized in terms of several key points. First, an authenticating mark of the church is its missionary consciousness, a sense of being mandated by Jesus Christ to continue his work of witnessing to the reign of God in the world. The Anabaptist movement bears the marks of a pentecostal irruption. Only such a pneumatological event had the potential to overturn the status quo. Second, the church must be animated by an awareness that it is God's new creation, the community that lives in submission to Jesus as *Kyrios*, rather than being socially conformed and compliant. Earthly powers, including the hierarchies of church and state, cannot make an absolute claim on the people of God. In the third place, effective missionary engagement depends on the message being effectively contextualized. The message of the sixteenth-century Anabaptists responded to the most basic issues confronting European society at that time, by providing both critique and a compelling alternative. Finally, the power of the Anabaptist witness lay in its insistence on recovery of the whole gospel that would be worked out in a life of discipleship that reflected the reign of God in every aspect of life: lifestyle, sociopolitical relations, witness to the world. The church was to be fully in the world but never subservient to it. This defining mark of the church was most evident in the way the community of disciples conducted all human relationships: the love ethic was to be the basis for human interaction both within the church and in the world.[50] This remains ever essential to authentic missionary witness and service, for it arises from the *missio Dei* (John 3:16–17).

---

[50] This is the third dimension of the Anabaptist vision as formulated by Bender, "Anabaptist Vision," 51.

# 2

## *Mennonites and the Evangelical Network*

After 1590, under pressure of relentless persecution and official suppression, the character of the Anabaptist movement was modified decisively. Descendants of the sixteenth-century Anabaptists had mutated into two distinct forms. In the Netherlands, leading Dutch Doopsgezinden became prosperous and joined the cultural mainstream. In Switzerland, Germany, and France, the move was toward cultural enclaves where Mennonites sought to preserve key spiritual values. In both cases, the original Anabaptist impulse to evangelize was effectively lost. In 1660 a Dutch Doopsgezind pastor, Thieleman J. van Braght, published his landmark book, *The Bloody Theater or Martyrs Mirror of the Defenseless Christians,* out of concern that his people had lost sight of their spiritual roots in a movement based on costly discipleship. While van Braght was grateful for the toleration that had come to Dutch society following the Thirty Years War, he observed that "toleration begat self-satisfaction, and self-satisfaction begat what he acutely sensed to be 'the absence of God.'"[1] Ultimately, what counted was a church consisting of committed disciples. Now the church needed a renewal of spiritual vitality. That renewal was to come by way of the Pietist movement in Germany and, subsequently, the evangelical revival in the Anglo-American world.

### EVANGELICAL ORIGINS

If Anabaptism was a force for church renewal in the sixteenth century, evangelicalism emerged late in the seventeenth century as the engine of revival. Unlike Anabaptism, which quickly was marginalized and officially censured, evangelicalism was tolerated—albeit often reluctantly—and exerted a leavening influence in the churches until the mid-nineteenth century, when a new wave of revival led to the formation of new denominational bodies with an explicit evangelical identity. The main exception to this generalization is the Wesleyan movement; yet until his death in 1791 John Wesley insisted that he had no intention of leaving the Church of England.

---

[1] Alan Kreider, "'The Servant Is Not Greater Than His Master': Anabaptists and the Suffering Church," *Mennonite Quarterly Review* 58 (January 1984): 25.

## *"Evangelical" Defined*

The word "evangelical" carries historical, theological, and ecclesiastical connotations. Menno Simons repeatedly contrasted "true evangelical faith"—that is, faith based on the Word alone—with formal religion that was the product of sacramentalism and sacerdotalism.[2] In contemporary English, the word "evangelical" is used in several senses. The term is included in the official names of various denominations—Evangelical Lutheran Church in America, for example—that typically have roots in Europe, where traditionally "evangelical" and "Protestant" have been used interchangeably. Historically, it refers to a renewal movement that started in late seventeenth-century Germany as Pietsm and was joined by the evangelical revival in the eighteenth century in Great Britain and North America. The Pietist/evangelical revival became an ecclesiastical stream that has had wide influence on western church life and, through the modern missionary movement, on the church worldwide. In North America in the twentieth century, it became common practice to use "evangelical" to describe mass or popular Christianity that is identified with contemporary Christian music, popular Christian magazines, radio and television stations, and celebrity Christian figures.

## *Pietism and Evangelicalism*

Evangelicalism arose as a renewal movement at a time when the great Volkskirchen appeared to be moribund. In 1675 Philip Jakob Spener published his *Pia Desideria,* the work that became the authoritative source for the Pietist movement. August Hermann Francke and Nikolaus Ludwig von Zinzendorf were the other outstanding Pietist leaders of the first generation. In the 1730s, a similar renewal movement associated with the names of Jonathan Edwards, George Whitefield, and John Wesley was kindled in North America and the British Isles. Although we speak of Pietism and the evangelical revival in the singular, it consisted of various strands reflecting local conditions and leaders. This movement proved to be highly fecund and was to become the source of a wide range of religious, social, and cultural innovations over the next century.

In contrast to the Volkskirchen, which were characterized by formalism and rationalism, especially under the impact of the Enlightenment, Pietists and evangelicals emphasized the personal and experiential, thus offering an attractive alternative to many people who

---

[2] See, e.g., John Christian Wenger, ed., and Leonard Verduin, trans., *The Complete Writings of Menno Simons* (Scottdale, Pa.: Herald Press, 1956), 343.

had become disaffected with the traditional church. But the Pietist/evangelical synthesis was not simply an ephemeral and emotional religious expression. It has been a decisive force in Christianity since the seventeenth century. A cluster of four features distinguishes evangelicalism from other Christian traditions. It is conversionist, activist, biblicist, and crucicentric.[3] These core values constitute its dynamic center. Evangelicalism has never overcome its initial self-understanding: from the beginning it was a movement of Christian renewal. The church was taken for granted and evangelical theology has failed to develop an effective ecclesiology. Evangelicals, ever animated by an activist spirit, have tended to work outside the church and create parachurch structures rather than revise and renew ecclesial forms to meet present needs.

It should come as no surprise that the modern mission movement, which emerged in the last years of the eighteenth century, was decidedly evangelical in motivation and character.[4] The roots of modern missions are to be found in Pietism and evangelicalism. Gustav Warneck asserted that "it was in the age of Pietism that missions struck their first deep roots, and it is the spirit of Pietism which, after Rationalism had laid its hoarfrost on the first blossoming, again revived them, and has brought them to their present bloom."[5] Even Roman Catholic missions that experienced a new beginning in the nineteenth century reflect the influence of evangelical Protestantism at this point.

To be sure, missions were but one aspect of an evangelicalism that was the dominant religious force in the British Isles and North America

---

[3] D. W. Bebbington, *Evangelicalism in Modern Britain: A History from the 1730s to the 1980s* (London: Unwin Hyman, 1989), 5–17.

[4] The modern mission movement was overwhelmingly evangelical in inspiration and implementation. The Anglo-Catholic societies founded around 1700 had lost steam, reflecting the moribund conditions of the mainstream Church of England (See H. P. Thompson, *Into All Lands: The History of the Society for the Propagation of the Gospel in Foreign Parts, 1701–1950* [London: SPCK, 1951], 104). The Roman Catholic missionary orders had been severely suppressed and curtailed by the Vatican with the dissolution of the Jesuits in 1773. Both traditions experienced revival in the wake of the evangelically-inspired missionary movement from 1792 onward.

[5] Gustav Warneck, *Outline of a History of Protestant Missions from the Reformation to the Present Time: A Contribution to Modern Church History*, trans. George Robson (New York: Fleming H. Revell Co., 1906), 53.

in the nineteenth century.[6] On the continent, Pietism made less impact but nonetheless had an important leavening influence through the work of such figures as the Blumhardts in Germany. A range of new Christian ministries and social witness resulted from nineteenth-century evangelical Pietism, because it successfully combined a biblical theology with a sense of responsibility to the world.[7]

In contrast to other Christian traditions, the evangelical identity has been substantially defined by its commitment to evangelism and missions. From the beginning, the modern mission movement captured the support of the evangelical constituency. It gave full scope to the activist and entrepreneurial spirit, and was based on a compelling biblical command that was focused in personal and social conversion. It appealed for the reclamation of "heathen" lands for Christ and his kingdom, and called for the fullest measure of heroic sacrifice ("my life, my all"). Missions and evangelism became the supreme measure of Christian devotion. Thus, the educational institutions established by evangelicals, especially Bible schools and colleges, were justified in terms of their role in training men and women for evangelization at home and missionary service abroad.

MENNONITE AMBIVALENCE TOWARD RENEWAL AND MISSIONS

From the historical record we can only conclude that Mennonites were ambivalent both about aspects of the renewal movement and, subsequently, about the budding missions movement.

This hesitation cannot be attributed solely to Mennonite isolation from these wider currents of spiritual rejuvenation. On the contrary, Mennonites felt the influence of Pietist and evangelical renewal

---

[6] See William G. McLoughlin, ed., *The American Evangelicals: 1800–1900* (New York: Harper & Row, 1968), 1: "The story of American Evangelicalism is the story of America itself in the years 1800 to 1900, for it was Evangelical religion which made Americans the most religious people in the world, molded them into a unified, pietistic-perfectionist nation, and spurred them on to those heights of social reform, missionary endeavor, and imperialistic expansionism which constitute the moving forces of our history in that century." This judgment has been echoed by other scholars. Cf. Leonard I. Sweet, "The Evangelical Tradition in America," chap. 1 in *The Evangelical Tradition in America* (Macon, Ga.: Mercer University Press, 1984).

[7] Dale W. Brown, *Understanding Pietism* (Grand Rapids: Wm. B. Eerdmans Co., 1978), 132–33.

movements in Europe and North America early.[8] Indeed, they found the call to spiritual renewal compelling. Like their Protestant neighbors, in the eighteenth century many Mennonite congregations were beset with a traditionalism—not always free of legalism—that was in danger of losing its grip on the loyalty of the younger generation. Mennonites had maintained their commitment to believers baptism, but its meaning was compromised by the fact that to a great extent it had become a mechanism for socializing youth into the church and keeping them within the traditional community. The evangelical call for personal responsibility based on a heart-felt conversion experience was a persuasive offer. Revival theology and methodology emphasized the importance of conversion and holy living, but revivalism also posed multiple threats to Mennonites. It was a force for both theological and cultural innovation that could be disruptive of the prized tight-knit community.

---

[8] See Harold S. Bender, "Revival," *The Mennonite Encyclopedia* (Scottdale, Pa.: Mennonite Publishing House; Newton, Kans.: Mennonite Publication Office; Hillsboro, Kans.: Mennonite Brethren Publishing House, 1959), 4:308–10; and Cornelius Krahn, "Pietism," *Mennonite Encyclopedia,* 4:176–79. Also, Richard K. MacMaster, *Land, Piety, Peoplehood: The Establishment of Mennonite Communities in America 1683–1790,* The Mennonite Experience in America, vol. 1 (Scottdale, Pa., and Kitchener, Ont.: Herald Press, 1985), 157–82, 206–28; Theron F. Schlabach, *Peace, Faith, Nation: Mennonites and Amish in Nineteenth-Century America,* The Mennonite Experience in America, vol. 2 (Scottdale, Pa., and Kitchener, Ont.: Herald Press, 1988), 22–32; Peter M. Friesen, *The Mennonite Brotherhood in Russia (1789–1910)* (Fresno, Calif.: Board of Christian Literature, 1980), 96, 100, 137–39, 141–42; Gerhard Lohrenz, "The Mennonites of Russia and the Great Commission," in *A Legacy of Faith: The Heritage of Menno Simons,* ed. C. J. Dyck (Newton, Kans.: Faith and Life Press, 1962), 175; Waldemar Janzen, "Foreign Mission Interest of the Mennonites in Russia before World War I," *Mennonite Quarterly Review* 42 (January 1968): 57–67; Orlando H. Wiebe, "The Missionary Emphasis of Pietism," in *The Church in Mission,* ed. A. J. Klassen (Hillsboro, Kans.: Mennonite Brethren Publishing House, 1967), 115–33; G. W. Peters, *Foundations of Mennonite Brethren Missions* (Hillsboro, Kans., and Winnipeg: Kindred Press, 1984), 16–28; Hans Kasdorf, *A Century of Mennonite Brethren Mission Thinking, 1885–1984* (Th.D. thesis, University of South Africa, 1986), chap. 4 and 5.

*Emergence of the Brethren*

To clarify this Mennonite ambivalence, we need to consider the threat Mennonites felt from the Pietists. One of the most important of these relationships was with the Brethren. This Brethren movement was born at Schwarzenau, Germany, in 1708. It was a movement motivated by the imperative to call people to the primitive faith of the first Christians. As was true in the sixteenth century, the church as a whole in the eighteenth century was deemed to be moribund. In Alexander Mack's earliest writing, *Basic Questions* (1713), the thirty-third question is: "Do you regard your church as superior to those of all other Baptist-minded *(Taufgesinnte)* of these or previous times, and if so, in which way and why?" Mack replies: "It is true that we consider our church fellowship superior to these now-deteriorated Baptists [Anabaptists]. Many of them notice this and realize it themselves."[9] As was true for the sixteenth-century Anabaptists, Mack based his call for vital faith and believers baptism on the Matthean and Markan versions of the Great Commission. And this led directly to Brethren efforts to evangelize their neighbors whose faith had grown formal and cold.

Persecution caused the Brethren to migrate from Germany to the United States. By 1729 the entire community had settled in Pennsylvania, with many Mennonite and Brethren communities intermingling. The renewal-minded Brethren disturbed the Mennonite bent toward maintaining the status quo.

Thus, North American Mennonite ambivalence toward Pietist/ evangelical influences becomes understandable. Mennonites could embrace spiritual renewal and might draw on evangelical resources in congregational life, especially adopting revival songs and new theological vocabulary. But Mennonites resisted until the mid-nineteenth

---

[9] Donald F. Durnbaugh, comp., *European Origins of the Brethren: A Source Book on the Beginnings of the Church of the Brethren in the Early Eighteenth Century* (Elgin, Ill.: Brethren Press, 1958), 340. Cf. Albert T. Ronk, *History of Brethren Missionary Movements* (Ashland, Ohio: Brethren Publishing Co., 1971), 9–11: "The same Mackian principle appears in the fact that an answer to another question about *true obedience*, shows in full acceptance of the Commission of Matthew 28:19, 20, to disciple and teach all nations full observance of the commands of Jesus. The command to teach is as strong as the command to baptize, and teaching *the nations* is mission of the highest order.... The consciousness of mission occupying the mind of the founding fathers was not purposefully expressed in their meager writings, but it is amply clear in what they did."

century other innovations that accompanied renewal: Sunday schools, worship in the English language, and articulated evangelistic methods.

## Pietist Influence on Mennonites in Europe and Russia

Cornelius Krahn held that "No other single religious movement has had such an impact on the Mennonites in all countries, with the exception of the Netherlands, as Pietism."[10] Pietist itinerant evangelists played a signal role in spreading the message of renewal from Germany eastward as far as Russia, using the network of congregational contacts they developed among Baptists, Lutherans, and Mennonites throughout the region. The impact of the Pietists was felt both in congregational life and in missionary outreach.[11]

Already by the nineteenth century, evangelicals and Pietists had an impressive international network of relationships built and nurtured by itinerant evangelists, Bible teachers, missionary societies, missionary training schools, social service institutions, and a plethora of magazines, pamphlets, and books in various languages. Three examples of Mennonite-evangelical interaction illustrate the character and reach of this network.

*1. Support of Russian Bible Society.* It has been reported that the Mennonites in Russia became early supporters of the Russian Bible Society, because this enabled them to participate in the evangelization of Russian peoples through Scripture distribution, something Mennonites were forbidden to do directly.[12] It should be noted that the founding of the St. Petersburg Bible Society in 1813 was part of a wider movement given impetus by the British and Foreign Bible Society (BFBS) that resulted in the formation of dozens of national or regional Bible societies. The BFBS was but one of many new societies formed at the initiative of a relatively small group of British evangelicals with large vision and useful connections at home and abroad.

The BFBS was organized in 1804 as a more specialized counterpart of the Religious Tract Society (founded in 1799). The Mennonite merchant in Altona, Germany, Jacob Gysberg van der Smissen (1746–1829) developed close ties to the BFBS and regularly contributed to its

---

[10] Krahn, "Pietism," *Mennonite Encyclopedia,* 4:176.

[11] Orlando H. Wiebe, "Missionary Emphasis of Pietism," 115–33, gives an overview of Pietist influences on Russian Mennonite life, including missionary outreach.

[12] Lohrenz, "Mennonites of Russia and the Great Commission," 176.

support. In 1809 he was elected an honorary governor of the society. His family maintained close ties with the society, and one of the younger van der Smissens served for several years on the staff of the BFBS in London.[13]

Among the prime movers in these initiatives was a young German Pietist pastor, C. F. A. Steinkopf, who had come to London in 1801 as pastor of the German Lutheran church at Savoy, London. Prior to moving to London, Steinkopf had been secretary of the Christian Society of Basel, which gave him experience with a variety of religious agencies. In London he quickly involved himself in expanding the work of these new societies internationally and was named foreign correspondent of the BFBS. In 1812 Steinkopf visited the continent for purposes of promoting the Bible cause, and traveled to Germany, Denmark, Sweden, and Switzerland. His travel diary reveals that twice on this trip he passed through Altona, where he was given hospitality by the van der Smissen family. Later Steinkopf returned to Germany to continue developing this international network of evangelical agencies. He itinerated across Europe and Russia, thus opening up opportunity for groups such as the Mennonites, who lacked their own facilities, to become involved in this growing movement.

*2. Support of Baptist Missions.* A second instance shows how Mennonites were introduced to the modern mission movement by some of its earliest leaders. At the urging of William Carey, the British Baptists had organized a missionary society in 1792. Carey went to India as the first Baptist missionary the following year, settling in the interior of Bengal and working as an indigo planter. In 1800 Carey moved to Serampore, where he was joined by other missionary colleagues. The Serampore Baptist mission soon became well known. The Baptist missionaries' reports were widely disseminated and attracted financial support from people in other countries, including Dutch Mennonites. In 1820 a Baptist delegation consisting of William Henry Angas (an English Baptist pastor and weighty member of the Baptist Missionary Society board), and missionary William Ward (on furlough from Serampore), visited the Netherlands to encourage formation of a BMS auxiliary for the purpose of raising support. By 1824 the Dutch Aid Society was formed, with Samuel Muller, eminent Mennonite pastor and

---

[13] William F. Mundt, *Sinners Directed to the Saviour: The Religious Tract Society Movement in Germany (1811–1848)* (Zoetermeer: Boekencentrum, 1996), 50. Mundt makes frequent references to van der Smissen.

seminary professor, as president. Mennonites were the mainstay of this society until 1847 when the Mennonites withdrew to form the Dutch Mennonite Missionary Association for the purpose of sending missionaries to the Dutch East Indies.[14]

Angas made a more extensive trip to the continent in 1824, visiting Mennonites in Prussia, Poland, Bavaria, the Palatinate, Switzerland, and France. As a result, regular mission offerings and an annual mission festival were instituted. In addition to funds raised for the Baptist mission, monies were also sent to the Berlin Missionary Society. In 1830 the Baptist Missionary Society appointed a German, the Rev. C. C. P. Tauchnitz, to represent them in Germany "in order to promote its objects on the Continent of Europe, and especially among the Mennonite Baptists."[15] Tauchnitz enjoyed good rapport with German Mennonites and made a constructive contribution to church life by helping them with some publishing projects, participating in renewal conferences, and encouraging theological training.

*3. Missionary Training.* A third example of Mennonite participation in this evangelical network is Samuel S. Haury. Born in Germany and brought to the United States by his parents as a child in 1856, Haury studied at Wadsworth Seminary in Ohio, where he was greatly influenced by C. J. van der Smissen. Van der Smissen, from the well-known van der Smissen family of Altona, Germany, had been shaped by Pietist influences, including study at the Basel Mission School, and he brought a passion for missions to his teaching. Upon graduation from Wadsworth Seminary in 1871 Haury went to Europe where he enrolled in the Rhenish Missionary Training School at Barmen and studied for the next four years. The Rhenish Mission had founded its great mission to Sumatra in 1861, and the school enjoyed a close link with its sponsoring society's emerging fields of missionary service. To read Haury's pamphlet, *Briefe über die Ausbreitung des Evangeliums in*

---

[14] Theodoor Erik Jensma, *Doopsgezinde Zending in Indonesië* ('s-Gravenhage: Boekencentrum, 1968), 1–9; S. F. Pannabecker, "Missions, Foreign Mennonite," *The Mennonite Encyclopedia* (Scottdale, Pa.: Mennonite Publishing House; Newton, Kans.: Mennonite Publication Office; Hillsboro, Kans.: Mennonite Brethren Publishing House, 1957), 3:713.

[15] Baptist Missionary Society Minutes, 8 July 1830, no. 20, 294. (I am indebted to Dr. A. Christopher Smith for providing this citation.) Christian Neff, "Tauchnitz, Carl Christian Philipp," *Mennonite Encyclopedia*, 4:685. Neff is silent about Tauchnitz's role as a missions promoter, leading one to suspect this portfolio on behalf of the BMS proved unworkable and was dropped.

*der Heidenwelt* (1877), written initially as a series of articles for *Der Mennonitische Friedensbote* a year after his return from Europe, is to savor Pietism's apology for missions. Haury made no attempt to clothe it in Mennonite garb.[16]

From the earliest years of the nineteenth century, Mennonites were exposed to the emerging missionary movement. They showed a certain interest but, significantly, took no initiative to sponsor such work on their own until after 1847. In that year, the Dutch Mennonites founded the first Mennonite mission board for foreign missions, the Dutch Mennonite Missionary Association. A key person in this development was the Dutch Mennonite businessman, C. P. van Eeghen, whose family was active in the Reveil (awakening) and in close touch with a network of like-minded folk in Great Britain and throughout the continent actively promoting new Christian initiatives.[17]

## MENNONITES AND THE MODERN MISSION MOVEMENT

The foregoing section has presented in broad strokes the historical trajectory that helped launch Mennonites into world mission. It is evident that evangelicalism furnished the motive power of this trajectory.[18] We

---

[16] See English edition, Samuel S. Haury, *Letters Concerning the Spread of the Gospel in the Heathen World Presented to All Mennonites in North America,* trans. Marie Regier Janzen and Hilda Voth (Scottdale, Pa.: Herald Press, 1981).

[17] Alle Hoekema, "Why the Dutch Were the First Mennonites to Send Missionaries Overseas," *Conrad Grebel Review* 15, no. 1/2 (winter/spring 1997): 23–34, traces the multiple influences and relationships that figure in this development. This case illustrates brilliantly the important role of these networks.

[18] Peters, *Foundations of Mennonite Brethren Missions,* 51, cites this summary by Samuel M. Zwemer, outstanding Reformed missionary in the Middle East, later professor at Princeton Theological Seminary, which gives classic expression to the evangelical vision of mission: "Apart from God in Christ there can be no missionary enterprise. In Jesus Christ the work of missions finds its basis, its aim, its method, its message, its motive, and its goal. The evangelization of the nations is not a human but a divine project—an eternal purpose of God which he purposed in Christ Jesus. The message of the New Testament to the heathen world was redemption from sin. The word of the Cross was the message of the apostles; the power of the Cross was their motive; and the glory of the resurrection was their hope." Peters comments: "The Mennonite Brethren Church would agree with Zwemer's statement without the slightest hesitation; it sums up decades of missions preaching in North America."

have emphasized that the modern missions movement sprang from the evangelical awakening. But the movement had a much wider impact. For example, historians argue that evangelical dynamism made it the dominant force among American Protestants for nearly a century—until the rise of the social gospel and theological modernism toward the end of the nineteenth century contributed to a breakdown of this consensus.[19]

The first Mennonite to be commissioned as a missionary in modern times, Pieter Jansz (1820–1904), is a prototype for Mennonite missionaries. Jansz and his wife were sent by the Dutch Mennonite Missionary Association to the Dutch East Indies in 1851. In his youth, he had come under the influence of the Reveil and identified with this movement in its emphasis on the new birth as the basis for true Christian faith.[20] Except for the matter of baptism, where he adhered to the traditional Mennonite insistence on adult baptism, Jansz's theology was Protestant orthodoxy with a bias toward Pietist expression. Jansz went to Java as a teacher, rather than as a professional missionary or pastor. He formed cordial and constructive working relations with missionary colleagues of other churches. Jansz was sensitive to the fact that theological debates in Europe over such questions as baptism might prove harmful to the young church in Java, but he was not trained as a theologian and brought little theological perspective to his work.

Like Pieter Jansz, the typical Mennonite missionaries had been touched by the evangelical revival and Protestant missionary movement and offered themselves for missionary service under the impetus of appeals such as "The evangelization of the world in this generation." Not a few Mennonite students felt the impact of the surging Student Volunteer Movement and its dynamic annual conventions. When Mennonite missionaries arrived in the country of assignment, they

---

[19] Although some modernists continued to support missions until the 1930s—the Hocking Report, *Rethinking Missions,* was published in 1932—no significant missionary initiative has ever emerged from this wing of the Protestant churches. Their program was to modernize, and thus modify (and neutralize?) the evangelical character of existing missions. This is consistent with John Kent's characterization of liberal theology as "parasitic" (*The End of the Line? The Development of Christian Theology in the Last Two Centuries* [Philadelphia: Fortress Press, 1982], 130); i.e., it has functioned as a reactive rather than generative agent since it operates out of the second, rather than first order.

[20] Alle Hoekema, "Pieter Jansz (1820–1904): First Mennonite Missionary to Java," *Mennonite Quarterly Review* 52 (January 1978): 70–71.

usually found a well-organized inter-mission system ready to help them get started. In a word, Mennonites were dependent on the wider mission movement. Several facets of this dependency can be identified.

In the first place, from the earliest years of the modern mission movement, an incipient ecumenism was evident, and in time this would mature into formal patterns and structures. Missions promoted positive ecclesiastical relations far in advance of their sending churches. In the field, it was assumed that missions would cooperate with one another. Toward the end of the nineteenth century, Protestants instituted the system of comity by which inter-mission relations were monitored and guided. By the time of the second wave of Mennonite mission expansion, 1890–1910, comity was taken for granted. In his history of mission comity, R. Pierce Beaver cites approvingly the way the Mennonites started work in Argentina in 1917, "by locating in an area where no other agency was at work."[21] This indicates that Mennonites accepted and cooperated with the system.

Second, Mennonites were late arrivals in virtually every country to which they went. The major Protestant bodies and Roman Catholic missions were widespread throughout Asia and Africa by the latter part of the nineteenth century, and the whole of Latin America was considered Roman Catholic. Mennonites were cast in the role of junior member of the missions community, a position reinforced by their typically being small in size when measured by the number of missionary staff and scale of program. That this status conferred certain advantages would only be discerned over time.

In the third place, Mennonites depended on the modern mission movement for the missiological framework within which they worked. They had developed no philosophy of mission of their own. When they began sending missionaries, they appropriated the philosophy that then guided all Protestant missions.[22] In this respect, Mennonites profited from the hard-won experience of others. At the beginning of the modern era, it was well recognized that no one understood adequately how best to go about the task of founding the church in diverse cultures. The first

---

[21] R. Pierce Beaver, *Ecumenical Beginnings in Protestant World Mission: A History of Comity* (New York: Thomas Nelson and Co., 1962), 155.

[22] See Personnel Manual, Mennonite Board of Missions and Charities (Elkhart, Ind., 1898), which appointed workers were required to sign. It states the aims and goals of missionary work. This "textbook" statement conformed to standard Protestant thinking.

two generations of mission leaders emphasized the importance of developing basic principles and methods by which to conduct the Christian mission. By the time Mennonites began sending out missionaries, a consensus had formed about the goal of mission, and a variety of methods had won approval. In the history of the period 1851–1945, one finds few examples of Mennonite thinking about the goals and methods of missions. The attitude seems to have been that the blueprints had been tested and were waiting to be applied wherever new opportunities arose. An exception to this generalization is Pieter Jansz. He wrestled with the problems of establishing the church in a resistant, even hostile, culture and wrote a book, *Land Reclamation and Evangelism in Java*, in which he advocated creation of Christian communities or colonies where young Christians might find support and protection.[23]

Mennonites turned to the established mission journals to furnish them with reports and interpretive articles on the burning issues of the day. In turn, they contributed little to missiological thought prior to 1950. They wrote no works on mission theory and practice.[24] They apparently were content to look to Kraemer, Zwemer, Speer, Mott, and others to generate the missiological capital on which the enterprise operated, as these leaders all worked out of a broadly evangelical framework.[25]

---

[23] Hoekema, "Pieter Jansz," 66–68. This idea was advocated by various people throughout the nineteenth century, especially when the young church was surrounded, as was frequently the case, by a hostile and threatening majority. Jansz did not think of this as a Mennonite solution. Mennonite missiological innovation would come only after 1950, and that particularly in relation to disadvantaged or exploited indigenous groups (e.g., the Choco of Panama, and Tobas of the Argentine Chaco), independent churches especially in Africa, and in the Middle East with its multiple tensions.

[24] See "Bibliography of Mennonite Missions," *Mission Focus* 12 (December 1984), the first attempt to compile a comprehensive bibliography of Mennonite and Brethren in Christ missions (exclusive of popular articles appearing in denominational or missionary agency periodicals). While incomplete, this compilation shows how little writing missionaries or mission executives did prior to 1945.

[25] In this respect they were clearly evangelical in their outlook. After the World Missionary Conference, Edinburgh, 1910, the conciliar or ecumenical movement began to emerge and the modernist-fundamentalist polarization resulted in separation between erstwhile allies. See the bibliographic overview of evangelical writings on missions which demonstrates that virtually all

Mennonites looked to this wider evangelical movement to provide strategic leadership in mission. Traditional Mennonitism was patently nonmissionary in outlook, and the "Anabaptist vision" lay more than a generation in the future. Except for medical doctors, Mennonite missionaries rarely had any advanced training. Thus, as members of a "sectarian" group and with inferior education, Mennonites were clearly at a disadvantage vis-à-vis the larger and long-established missions.

A fourth characteristic, one arising from the Mennonite tradition of a lay untrained ministry, was the Mennonite reluctance to found theological schools. Even the Dutch Mennonites, who alone of all European and American Mennonites had a seminary before 1860, having founded one in 1735, did not establish a seminary as a part of their church development in the Dutch East Indies. Given the scope of Mennonite mission work since 1851, it is noteworthy how few advanced-level theological training schools Mennonites have founded.[26]

Mennonite missions favored Bible schools that trained evangelists, catechists, and lay people. The select few who were sent on for advanced theological training got it in one of three kinds of programs: (1) a seminary of another denomination or interdenominational group, (2) a specially organized temporary training program set up for a particular group of students, or (3) a cooperative theological education program that Mennonites co-sponsored. For example, the Dutch Mennonite Mission cooperated in the formation of the ecumenical Higher Theological School, Jakarta, Indonesia, in the mid-1930s. S. Djojodihardjo (1918–88), outstanding long-time leader of the Javanese Mennonites, was a member of the first HTS graduating class. No attempt at evaluation of this Mennonite missions policy has been made, but surely it has had important consequences. At a minimum, this practice effectively handed over to other denominations and traditions responsibility for shaping the identity of these "new" Mennonites.

---

*scholarly* evangelical missiological work has appeared since 1945; in Wilbert R. Shenk, "North American Evangelical Missions since 1945: A Bibliographic Survey," in *Earthen Vessels: American Evangelicals and Foreign Missions, 1880–1980,* ed. Joel A. Carpenter and Wilbert R. Shenk (Grand Rapids: Wm. B. Eerdmans Co., 1990), 317–34.

[26] See survey by Erland Waltner, "Seminaries," *The Mennonite Encyclopedia,* (Scottdale, Pa., and Waterloo, Ont.: Herald Press, 1990), 5:809–11.

MENNONITES IN ASIA, AFRICA, AND LATIN AMERICA

Thus far we have been concerned with Mennonite-evangelical interaction in Europe and North America. The main argument has been that evangelicalism was the catalytic agent that caused Mennonites finally to join the modern mission movement toward the end of the nineteenth century. In taking this crucial step, Mennonites held on to the formal structure of their tradition, while allowing the evangelical dynamic to redefine and redirect their church life. The bias of the Mennonite tradition was self-preservation rather than mission; evangelicalism had a decided activist/missional thrust. It was taken for granted that to find a serviceable theology and philosophy of missions, Mennonites had to turn to the evangelical movement. Thus, the Mennonite tradition was retained as the husk of the evangelical kernel.[27] But these two dimensions have not always fit together harmoniously.

Whatever their appearance, the vitality of Mennonite missions reflected the evangelical dynamic rather than the Mennonite tradition. To anyone who is familiar with the history of Christian missions in the modern period, this comes as no surprise. It can be demonstrated from a multitude of cases that attempts to indigenize western ecclesiastical traditions in Asia, Africa, and Latin America—with attention typically fixed on form and structure—have proved to be uniformly difficult and largely sterile exercises. Traditional Mennonite theology, which evolved as a means of holding the faith community together by keeping the world at bay, had little potential as the foundation for a theology of mission. By contrast, Anabaptist theology that arose as a prophetic protest against the spiritual sterility of the religious status quo could have been of considerable service, had it but been available at this time.

The first Mennonite missionaries who had been directly influenced by the historical/theological movement of "recovery of the Anabaptist vision" were not appointed until about 1950.[28] Even at this stage, the

---

[27] The leitmotiv of Theron F. Schlabach's *Gospel Versus Gospel: Mission and the Mennonite Church* (Scottdale, Pa.: Herald Press, 1980) is his criticism of Mennonite missionaries for borrowing so heavily from evangelical Protestants, a critique one can appreciate. However, it would have taken someone of extraordinary insight and perspective to see the missionary potential in a tradition forged as protective armor against external threat and designed to guard against a hostile world rather than lead to engagement with it.

[28] The first major scholarly address of the missionary dimension of the Anabaptist movement is that of Franklin H. Littell in 1946, republished as chapter 1 in *Anabaptism and Mission*, ed. Wilbert R. Shenk (Scottdale, Pa., and

missional implications of the Anabaptist heritage were not being mined for the benefit of Mennonite missionaries. (The Anabaptist vision was viewed primarily as the basis for a revitalization of traditional Mennonitism, not of mission.) Thus, we may conclude that the third phase of Mennonite missionary expansion, the post–World War 2 period, 1945–1965, remained essentially evangelical in character.

As a result, at the end of the twentieth century, by virtue of the character of the modern mission movement and the sheer numbers of people who have been added to the Mennonite family since 1965, the global Mennonite identity was more firmly evangelical than ever. This statement must, of course, be interpreted. "Evangelical" is a term of variegated meaning and it takes on distinctive coloration depending on locale. Rather than seeing Mennonite identity these past twenty-five years as evolving toward greater clarity and unity, we would do well to recognize that it has become ever more complex. To the pluriformity of evangelicalism must be added the evolving meaning of "Mennonite" and the confused attempts to give an Anabaptist patina to the whole.[29] Some of the theological ferment and development in Mennonite thought in Europe and North America stirred by the recovery of the Anabaptist vision since 1945 have found their way to Asia, Africa, and Latin America. However, this has remained largely an intellectual movement which has yet to take root in congregational life and discipleship.

Mennonite identity in Asia, Africa, and Latin America is being defined and redefined through several streams of influence. This process includes three important components: (1) the evangelical network, (2) the theological schools where leaders are being trained, and (3) the literature used for nurture and theological development.

---

Kitchener, Ont.: Herald Press, 1984), 13–23, and more fully in Littell's *The Origins of Sectarian Protestantism: A Study of the Anabaptist View of the Church* (New York: Macmillan, 1964). See the introduction to *Anabaptism and Mission* for an overview of scholarship on the theme, a theme that remains marginal to contemporary Anabaptist studies.

[29] The historico-theological nexus linking Anabaptists and Mennonites is frequently described in confusing or loose terms. See John H. Yoder, "Anabaptist Vision and Mennonite Reality," in *Consultation on Anabaptist-Mennonite Theology,* ed. A. J. Klassen (Fresno, Calif.: Council of Mennonite Seminaries, 1970), 1–46; and Wilbert R. Shenk, "A Developing Missiological Vision for Anabaptists," in *A Relevant Anabaptist Missiology for the 1990s,* ed. Calvin E. Shenk (Elkhart, Ind.: Council of International Ministries, 1990), 43–45. See also chapter 6 in this book.

*The Evangelical Network*

If one inquires about the key theological ideas that define these newer Mennonite churches, in most cases the answer will not be in terms of themes important to traditional Mennonite theology. It could hardly have been otherwise, because evangelicalism supplied the vocabulary and grammar by which these Mennonites first learned Christ, and it has provided the curriculum that has nurtured them since.

In India, for example, the Evangelical Fellowship of India (EFI) was organized in 1951, patterned after both the World Evangelical Fellowship and the (American) National Association of Evangelicals, but different at a crucial point. From the outset, the EFI did not force its members to choose between EFI and membership in the National Christian Council of India. Indeed, some EFI leaders continued to be officeholders in the NCCI. In addition to an annual convention, the EFI organized committees on evangelism, theological education, and literature. Later other committees, such as the Committee on Relief, were added. The EFI continually promoted prayer for revival of Christian life in India.[30] Mennonites joined in organizing and supporting the EFI from the beginning. EFI became a model of a moderate and irenic evangelicalism that held to its convictions without breaking fellowship with other Christian traditions. Not all regional or national evangelical fellowships assumed this conciliatory stance.

Since the 1960s, evangelicalism itself has undergone something of a renewal—theological, organizational, and spiritual—giving it a new dynamic and depth which it had not had since the nineteenth century. When mainstream Protestants formed the International Missionary Council in 1921, evangelicals, overshadowed by the modernist-fundamentalist controversy, declined to join. Only in the 1960s did evangelicals launch a series of international consultations and congresses on world evangelization and mission that have changed the movement in important ways. First, these events provided opportunity for articulate and able men and women from Asia, Africa, and Latin America to share in leadership of the world evangelical movement. Second, this broadened leadership has brought a new theological agenda: social justice, violence and nonviolence, the scope of the gospel, sociopolitical systems, and race

---

[30] See Robert J. McMahon, *To God Be the Glory: An Account of the Evangelical Fellowship of India's First Twenty Years, 1951–71* (New Delhi: Masihi Sahitya Sanstha, 1970), 1–12.

relations have all become matters of concern.[31] Third, the evangelical movement has refurbished and extended its network.

Two international organizations symbolize the "new" evangelical reality: World Evangelical Fellowship (WEF) and the Lausanne Continuation Committee—an extension of the landmark 1974 Lausanne Congress.[32] Many Mennonites in Asia, Africa, and Latin America have benefited from consultations, congresses, training schools, and seminars sponsored by evangelical organizations. At a time when many of the conciliar bodies are in decline, the evangelical network provides welcome opportunities for regional or international contacts, fellowship, and training. Neither conciliar nor Mennonite denominational opportunities have matched those afforded by the evangelical network.[33]

*Theological Training*

The ambivalent attitude of Mennonite missions toward advanced theological education has left a legacy among the Mennonite churches in Asia, Africa, and Latin America. Surveying the theological schools sponsored by Mennonites on these three continents, we conclude that only the Mennonite Brethren Seminary in Osaka, Japan, offers theological training in a Masters of Divinity program. Two Mennonite seminaries train students at the Bachelors in Theology level, and Mennonite churches sponsor a number of Bible schools.

---

[31] We lack a single comprehensive survey of these developments. Important facets are covered in chapters by Pierard, Van Engen, and Costas, in *Earthen Vessels,* ed. Carpenter and Shenk.

[32] See David M. Howard, *The Dream That Would Not Die: The Birth and Growth of the World Evangelical Fellowship, 1846–1986* (Exeter: Paternoster Press, 1986), for the WEF. Nothing comparable on the Lausanne movement is yet available, but see J. D. Douglas, ed., *Let the Earth Hear His Voice* (Minneapolis: Worldwide Publications, 1975), official proceedings of the International Congress on World Evangelization (including the Lausanne Covenant).

[33] It might be argued that the Mennonite World Conference is increasingly providing such a forum. The periodic MWC assemblies are of a different character, however, than the typical evangelical conference. The latter is normally organized around a carefully defined theme with emphasis on some aspect of world evangelization and how to accomplish it. MWC is designed for fellowship and mutual encouragement, rather than for promoting a specific program. MWC assemblies have the character of folk festivals rather than task-oriented consultations.

On the other hand, Mennonites cooperate in sponsoring a number of graduate seminaries in Africa and Asia. Except for the case of Indonesia, where the Mennonite churches participate in several ecumenical theological schools at the graduate level, all other associations are with evangelical seminaries or faculties of theology. In none of these institutions is there a program of Anabaptist/Mennonite studies. The curriculum typically is designed to be broadly acceptable to evangelicals. Evangelicals maintain a strong emphasis on evangelization and this influence continues to bear fruit in the growth of the churches through witness to the wider community. But since the nineteenth century, the evangelical tradition has been criticized for its lack of attention to ecclesiology. The evidence suggests that cooperative seminaries feel no strong mandate to emphasize ecclesiology, out of fear that this might undermine cooperation. One wonders how theological creativity can flourish without a solid grounding of the entire enterprise in ecclesial reality.

An important and instructive exception to this generalization is the Anabaptist Ministerial Leaders Seminary (SEMILLA) based in Guatemala, an innovative institution using the methodology of the Theological Education by Extension (TEE) movement. Several points should be noted. In the first place, SEMILLA has succeeded in establishing a program that serves the needs of the churches in several Central American countries, and this has contributed to a regional identity. Second, it has consciously tried to develop an Anabaptist identity in a region that has been in the throes of political and economic turmoil for more than two decades, a region where many ordinary people experience persecution and live in the shadow of martyrdom. It must be remembered that the evangelical movement has grown substantially in Latin America since the 1950s, with some evangelicals rising in political and military ranks. Leading evangelicals have aligned themselves with the ruling powers, while some of the most vigorous opposition has come from those Roman Catholics who have renounced their traditional alliance with the military-government establishment and become proponents of liberation theology. A third observation is that SEMILLA has succeeded in keeping the program attuned to the grassroots ecclesial reality.[34] A situation of oppression means the church is under constant

---

[34] In a personal communication (March 15, 1993) Amzie Yoder of the SEMILLA staff reported that this third concern is the most important, because of outside competition. SEMILLA's attempt to maintain an Anabaptist focus is

pressure to conform to the political-military powers or pay the price of noncompliance.

*Literature*

As noted above with reference to the founding of the Evangelical Fellowship of India in 1951, one of the committees established at the outset was literature. The churches of Asia, Africa, and Latin America have felt the lack of materials for Christian education and personal devotion as a result of such obstacles as lack of finances, inadequate distribution channels, poor production facilities, and shortage of writers and editors. Mennonites have contributed to the production of literature in many countries. Often they have done so in cooperation with evangelicals who have led the way in producing and publishing a range of materials for the Christian home and church. But Mennonites have written few works of theology or biblical studies in the languages indigenous to Asia, Africa, or Latin America. And this is not unique to Mennonites. Evangelical publishers have relied to a great extent on books written by Europeans or Americans and translated into other languages. This leads to several problems. At a time when it is widely agreed that theology should be contextualized, this perpetuates dependence on foreign theology. It also stifles serious theological reflection and interaction on the part of pastor and theologian. Beyond this, it often means that a kind of censorship has been practiced so that a publisher imports only those works that conform to a particular theological position. In the long term, this can have enormous consequences for formation of the theological identity of a church. This, of course, is precisely why some groups have seized the opportunity to specialize in the publication and distribution of Christian literature and books throughout the world.

---

questioned by North American Mennonites/Brethren in Christ, on the one hand, and evangelicals and pentecostals, on the other. "The electronic church, primarily from North America, is also constantly bombarding Central America with an individualized, spiritualized Gospel that alienates from the realities here." These North American churches seem to be oblivious to the neo-Constantinianism they are promoting.

CONCLUSION

In this chapter, we have surveyed the relationship between Mennonites and evangelicals. It is no more than a rough sketch. For example, we have not traced the role of renewal movements in the newer churches. One of the outstanding examples is the East African Revival that started in Uganda in 1929 and rapidly spread throughout the region. Its theological roots are in the Keswick Movement and the sociocultural context of colonial East Africa. It has penetrated the Mennonite churches in East Africa. In the 1960s and 1970s, the charismatic movement touched Mennonite churches in many countries on all continents. Each of these movements has further qualified the relationship between Mennonites and evangelicalism.

# 3

## Mission, Service, and the Globalization of North American Mennonites

INTRODUCTION

During the past century, North America Mennonites and Brethren in Christ have experienced an extraordinary permutation in identity. The primary sources of this development are the modern mission movement—which itself was entering a new phase of development by 1880—and the ministries of compassion that emerged out of emergency relief and development following World War 1. But this transformation needs to be placed within a wider frame. It is also a result of the all-encompassing globalization that has increasingly bound the world together. The process has been described as consisting of three stages: deprovincialization, internationalization, and globalization.[1] The journey through each stage is filled with struggle and strain as the old is forced to make way for the new. In addition, the modern project has been marked by profound ambiguity and contradiction for the church, as well as for humankind generally.

For Mennonites the process took direct and tangible forms. The first venture in organized mission for General Conference Mennonites began in the early 1880s, when Samuel and Susie Haury left Halstead, Kansas, to establish a mission to the Arapahos and Cheyennes in Oklahoma. James Juhnke has calculated that by 1900 more than one hundred Mennonites from sheltered rural communities, many without professional training or expertise, had rendered service through this mission in a variety of roles. The General Conference mission board publicized the mission widely and raised substantial financial and material support. "The mission became the cutting edge of the church," Juhnke has argued, "a magnet to attract and challenge the brightest

Reprinted with permission, with changes, from *Mennonite Quarterly Review* 70 (January 1996): 7–22.

[1] Max L. Stackhouse, "Globalization and Theology in America Today," in *World Order and Religion,* ed. Wade Clark Roof (Albany: State University of New York Press, 1991), 247–57.

young people moving out from Mennonite farms."[2] After twenty years the benefits derived by the Arapahos and Cheyennes from this outpouring were painfully meager and ambiguous, but the impact on the General Conference Mennonite Church was considerable. Not least, three future presidents of General Conference higher educational institutions were nurtured by their experiences with the mission. And having answered the call to mission among a people strange to them, members of the General Conference Mennonite Church had set out on the road toward deprovincialization.

## THE MENNONITE "GREAT CENTURY"

In his study of the background to the organization of the Mennonite Central Committee, written for the fiftieth anniversary of MCC in 1970, Guy F. Hershberger argued persuasively:

> The founding of the Mennonite Central Committee in 1920 represents an important milestone in the total sweep of Mennonite history, bearing a twofold symbolic significance. Looking backward from that date, we see it symbolizes the recovery of the Anabaptist vision of mission and service; looking forward, it symbolizes the opening of the door to a greater world-wide Mennonite brotherhood united in that mission and service to the modern world. In the half century preceding 1920 Mennonites were engaged in the solid task of recovery. The succeeding fifty years were given to the implementation of that mission which in 1970 was approaching maturity.[3]

However, this astute summary must be augmented at two points: (1) the considerable Mennonite debt to other Christian traditions for the help received during this transition must be reckoned with, and (2) the influence of sociopolitical forces on Mennonites should be assessed.

Conditions among Mennonites in North America during the nineteenth century have been well described by others.[4] In brief,

---

[2] James C. Juhnke, "General Conference Mennonite Missions to the American Indians in the Late Nineteenth Century," *Mennonite Quarterly Review* 54 (April 1980): 117.

[3] Guy F. Hershberger, "Historical Background to the Formation of the Mennonite Central Committee," *Mennonite Quarterly Review* 44 (July 1970): 213.

[4] See Frank H. Epp, *Mennonites in Canada, 1786–1920: The History of a Separate People* (Toronto: Macmillan of Canada, 1974); Frank H. Epp, *Mennonites in Canada, 1920–1940: A People's Struggle for Survival* (Scottdale, Pa.: Herald Press, 1982); Theron F. Schlabach, *Peace, Faith, Nation:*

Mennonites had long lived out of an enclave mentality that guided them in conserving their most cherished value: separation from the world in tight-knit communities. External forces, both secular and religious, constantly challenged these enclaves. For the most part, Mennonites responded to these outside influences defensively. As the century wore on, North American Mennonites were gradually drawn out of their traditional seclusion into worldwide engagement. Change came in a torrent of innovations between 1865 and 1918: a shift from German to English as the primary language of home and worship; the introduction of Sunday schools, revival meetings, home and foreign missions, educational institutions, deaconess work, emergency relief and mutual aid organizations; and increasing entrance into the professions. Three conflicts exerted crucial influence on North American Mennonites and Brethren in Christ in the twentieth century: the modernist-fundamentalist controversy and the two great world wars.

Mennonite involvement in mission during this period of cultural transformation divides readily into the three phases noted earlier: deprovincialization, 1880–1918; internationalization, 1918–1970; and globalization, 1970 to the present.

## 1880–1918: DEPROVINCIALIZATION

The period between 1880 and 1914 is sometimes called the "high imperial" era. A defining event was a conference of European powers, held in Berlin at the end of 1884 and early in 1885 for the purpose of dividing the continent of Africa into colonies. Imbued with the spirit of the Enlightenment and confident of the superiority of its values and

---

*Mennonites and Amish in Nineteenth-Century America,* The Mennonite Experience in America, vol. 2 (Scottdale, Pa., and Kitchener, Ont.: Herald Press, 1988); and James C. Juhnke, *Vision, Doctrine, War: Mennonite Identity and Organization in American 1890–1930,* The Mennonite Experience in America, vol. 3 (Scottdale, Pa., and Waterloo, Ont.: Herald Press, 1989), chap. 1–7. Important background on the mission movement among Mennonites is given in G. W. Peters, *Foundations of Mennonite Brethren Missions* (Hillsboro, Kans., and Winnipeg: Kindred Press, 1984); James C. Juhnke, *A People of Mission* (Newton, Kans.: Faith and Life Press, 1979); Theron F. Schlabach, *Gospel Versus Gospel: Mission and the Mennonite Church* (Scottdale, Pa.: Herald Press, 1980); and Lois Barrett, *The Vision and the Reality: The Story of Home Missions in the General Conference Mennonite Church* (Newton, Kans.: Faith and Life Press, 1983).

culture, the West believed itself destined to have charge of the "lesser peoples" of the world.

Although not directly involved in the first phase of high imperialism, Americans across the Atlantic were not immune to the allure of the imperial spirit. One of the most influential books of the day was Josiah Strong's *Our Country: Its Possible Future and Its Present Crisis,* published in 1886.[5] Strong skillfully blended religion and politics in an amalgam that undergirded the divinely-appointed mission of the Anglo-Saxon peoples to the rest of the world. He called for expansion and outreach on all fronts—political, military, cultural, commercial, and religious. The book became a powerful influence, propelling the people of the United States out of their cultural provincialism toward greater world involvement.

Before the end of the nineteenth century, the United States had gone to war against Spain in the Caribbean and the Philippine Islands in a crusade with both geopolitical and religious dimensions. Although a latecomer, the United States had now joined the ranks of the colonial powers. When the Ecumenical Missionary Conference was held in New York in April 1900, former U.S. president Benjamin Harrison, honorary chairman of the conference, delivered the opening address. President William McKinley, who led the United States into war against Spain,

---

[5] Josiah Strong, *Our Country: Its Possible Future and Present Crisis* (New York: Baker & Taylor, 1885). Strong was on the staff of the American Home Missionary Society at the time of writing the book. Subsequently he was general secretary of the Evangelical Alliance of the United States. In the preface to the revised edition of 1891, he reported that 130,000 copies of the first edition were in print and large parts of it had been serialized in newspapers throughout the U.S. and Canada. Special editions were published in Great Britain and it had been translated into one foreign language, with other translations pending. (It was translated into German and published by the Christliche Central-Buchhandlung, Berne, Ind., in 1892, which suggests that it had a certain appeal for Mennonites.) Strong was an ardent and articulate exponent of a surging nationalism, which he believed could be made to serve Christian ends. He said: "Our plea is not America for America's sake; but America for the world's sake. For, if this generation is faithful to its trust, America is to become God's right arm in his battle with the world's ignorance and oppression and sin" (New York: Baker & Taylor, 1891), 263. Historians have been severe in their criticism of Strong. But see Dorothea R. Muller, "Josiah Strong and American Nationalism: A Reevaluation," in *Missions and Ecumenical Expressions,* ed. Martin E. Marty (Munich, New York: K. G. Saur, 1993), 48–64; first published in *The Journal of American History* 53 (December 1966): 487–503.

and Governor Theodore Roosevelt of New York State, a hero of the Spanish-American war, also spoke during the inaugural session.[6] An estimated 20,000 people thronged the conference, which lasted for two weeks.

The very term "world war" conjures up an image that differs from our picture of regional or bilateral conflicts. Such a war engulfs the whole. World War 1, 1914–1918, put an end to the doctrine of progress that undergirded modern western culture throughout the nineteenth century, and it solidified the budding nationalist movements among peoples colonized by the European powers. The West was no longer regarded as invincible. This, too, was a part of the deprovincialization process, with direct implications for international relations.

Up to the 1880s the churches in the United States had been largely preoccupied with mission to the frontier areas of their own country, with the result that American church membership grew from about 7 percent of the population in 1800 to some 36 percent a century later. Now the angle of their mission vision was about to be shifted.[7]

---

[6] In his address, McKinley said: "I am glad of the opportunity to offer without stint my tribute of praise and respect to the missionary effort which has wrought such wonderful triumphs for civilization.... The missionary, of whatever church or ecclesiastical body, who devotes his life to the service of the Master and of men, carrying the torch of truth and enlightenment, deserves the gratitude, the support, the homage of mankind.... Wielding the sword of the Spirit, they have conquered ignorance and prejudice. They have been among the pioneers of civilization. They have illumined the darkness of idolatry and superstition with the light of intelligence and truth.... Who can estimate their value to the progress of nations? Their contribution to the onward and upward march of humanity is beyond all calculation." Quoted from *Ecumenical Missionary Conference, New York, 1900: Report of the Ecumenical Conference on Foreign Missions, Held in Carnegie Hall and Neighboring Churches, April 21 to May 1* (New York: American Tract Society, 1900), 1:39–40.

[7] For North American churches, unlike for European ones, mission did begin at home, in the seventeenth century, with the establishment of missions to the indigenous peoples. Historians such as Kenneth Scott Latourette have argued that the greatest mission success story in the nineteenth century was the evangelization of the United States. See Kenneth Scott Latourette, *The Great Century: Europe and the United States,* vol. 4 of *A History of the Expansion of Christianity* (New York: Harper & Bros., 1941; reprint, Grand Rapids: Zondervan, 1970). John K. Fairbank noted the simultaneous movement in the nineteenth century into foreign and home missions, but with the bulk of resources going into home missions until the rise of the Student Volunteer

In the summer of 1886 evangelist Dwight L. Moody, in association with the Intercollegiate Young Men's Christian Association (YMCA), hosted a meeting for students at Northfield, Massachusetts. This marked the start of the Student Volunteer Movement for Foreign Missions (SVM). The movement quickly caught the imagination of students on campuses throughout North America, and spread to Europe and several Asian countries. The SVM took as its slogan "The Evangelization of the World in This Generation." Controversial and criticized from the outset, the slogan nonetheless galvanized an entire generation of students because it effectively caught the mood of the times. Student Volunteer Bands were organized on college campuses to recruit volunteers and to provide moral and spiritual support for those who had already signed the pledge: "It is my purpose, if God permits, to become a foreign missionary." Fortunate to have outstanding leaders such as John R. Mott, Robert E. Speer, Robert P. Wilder, and G. Sherwood Eddy, the SVM was instrumental in recruiting more than 25,000 university graduates for world mission—largely from North America—by 1925. Indeed, already in 1900 the United States had surpassed the long-dominant British in the number of missionaries serving abroad. This was a powerful incoming tide.

The multiple facets of Mennonite and Brethren in Christ dependence on the Protestant missionary movement constitute a story that deserves to be told comprehensively.[8] It has various roots, including European Pietism,[9] American revivalism, and the holiness movement.

---

Movement ("Assignment for the '70's," *The American Historical Review* 74 [February 1969]: 876–79).

[8] Theron F. Schlabach, *Gospel Versus Gospel,* subjects the Mennonite Church mission movement to sustained critique because of this borrowing and dependency. The analysis needs to be extended to the entire Brethren in Christ and Mennonite family.

[9] See Samuel S. Haury, *Letters Concerning the Spread of the Gospel in the Heathen World Presented to All Mennonites in North America,* trans. Marie Regehr Janzen and Hilda Voth (Scottdale, Pa.: Herald Press, 1981; German original 1877); Orlando H. Wiebe, "The Missionary Emphasis of Pietism," in *The Church in Mission,* ed. A. J. Klassen (Fresno, Calif.: Board of Christian Literature, Mennonite Brethren Church, 1967), 115–33; G. W. Peters, *Foundations of Mennonite Brethren Missions* (Hillsboro, Kans., and Winnipeg: Kindred Press, 1984), chap. 1–2; and most comprehensively, Hans Kasdorf, *A Century of Mennonite Brethren Mission Thinking, 1885–1984* (Th.D. thesis, University of South Africa, 1986), chap. 3–4.

But, most obviously, Mennonite understandings of mission were shaped and guided by mainstream Protestant missions.

The first Mennonite Brethren missionaries to the nonwestern world were Abram and Mary Friesen from the Ukraine, who went to India in 1889. The Friesens spent four years preparing for missionary service at the Hamburg Baptist Seminary. Convinced of their call, in 1888 the Friesens appealed to the Mennonite Brethren Church in Russia for support. In their letter they said: "To organize an independent work we are too weak but we are able to develop in association with a Baptist mission a work among the poor heathen that will really prove a blessing if we but concentrate our whole strength upon a single point and send out our own workers into the already white harvest fields."[10] Mennonites were well aware of their small size and late arrival on the scene of foreign missions. But the American Baptist Missionary Union, Boston, willingly entered into agreement with the Mennonite Brethren. Within two years after the Friesens arrived in India, the Baptists ceded full responsibility to the Mennonites for the Nalgonda area.[11]

The conceptual dependence of early Mennonite missions can be demonstrated at a number of points. Noah E. Byers became principal of Elkhart Institute (forerunner of Goshen College) in 1898, following study at Northwestern University, where he was active in the YMCA. Immediately upon his arrival at the Elkhart Institute, Byers organized the Young People's Christian Association and encouraged the organization of the Student Volunteer Band the following year. Both organizations were influential on campus. In addition, students began attending the conventions of both the YMCA/YWCA and SVM, where they heard the challenge to world evangelization from John R. Mott, Robert E. Speer, Samuel Zwemer and others.[12] Mott's book, *The Evangelization of the*

---

[10] Quoted in G. W. Peters, *The Growth of Foreign Missions in the Mennonite Brethren Church* (Hillsboro, Kans.: Board of Foreign Missions, Conference of the Mennonite Brethren Church of North America, 1952), 57.

[11] The Mennonite missionaries organized a Mennonite Brethren Church in 1891. The cooperative arrangements with the Baptists continued until World War 1. The war made it impossible for funds to be sent from Russia. The Russian Revolution in 1917 forced the termination of the relationship and the Nalgonda work was integrated into the Baptist mission and church.

[12] At the time of Byer's involvement, John R. Mott was executive director of the YMCA as well as a major figure in the Student Volunteer Movement. For an account of Byers and his promotion of missions, see Susan Fisher Miller,

*World in This Generation* (1900),[13] was the basic text for the Mission Study Class, which attracted good enrollments.

When the first three missionaries were appointed for service in India by the Mennonite Evangelizing and Benevolence Board[14] in November 1898 they signed a personnel manual that defined their duties and relationships. Article fourteen spelled out the goal of their work:

> The raising up of self-supporting and self-extending churches must ever be kept in view. Converts must be stimulated and encouraged in the study of the Word of God; suitable opportunities should be afforded them for the manifestation of spiritual gifts; and they should be encouraged to help pecuniarily, according to their ability, in the work of God. Native helpers especially should be afforded all possible help and encouragement; as they become able they should be allowed to bear responsibility, and the element of foreign teaching, pastoral care, and supervision be gradually withdrawn. [15]

This was classic Protestant mission theory and policy, as developed over the previous century. Mennonite and Brethren in Christ missionaries would indeed take it to heart. Recent studies of Brethren in Christ missions in Zimbabwe (founded 1898), Zambia (founded 1906), and India (founded 1913) show how thoroughly the classical Protestant model was adopted and followed with virtually no modification until independent churches emerged in the 1960s.[16]

Three Mennonites attended the landmark World Missionary Conference in Edinburgh, Scotland, in June 1910. They were J. S. Shoemaker, secretary of the Mennonite Board of Missions and Charities, a delegate; and observers J. S. Hartzler, from the faculty of Goshen College, and Alfred Wiebe, a General Conference Mennonite applicant

---

*Culture for Service: A History of Goshen College, 1894–1994* (Goshen, Ind.: Goshen College, 1994), 24–31.

[13] John Raleigh Mott, *The Evangelization of the World in this Generation* (New York: Student Volunteer Movement for Foreign Missions, 1900).

[14] In 1906, the board merged with the Mennonite Board of Charitable Homes and Missions to become the Mennonite Board of Missions and Charities.

[15] Personnel Manual, Mennonite Board of Missions and Charities (Elkhart, Ind., 1898).

[16] See Harvey R. Sider, "From Mission to Church: India"; H. Frank Kipe, "From Mission to Church: Zambia and Zimbabwe"; and Wilbert R. Shenk, "From Mission to Church: A Response"; in *Brethren in Christ History and Life* 17 (August 1994): 113–72.

for missionary service.[17] Whereas the Mennonites represented agencies
with scarcely a decade of missionary work abroad, for the major
Protestant missions, with a century of work behind them, Edinburgh
marked a shift in focus from mission to church. One of the eight
commissions around which the conference was organized was "The
Church in the Mission Field."[18] As the report makes clear, one could now
speak of "the church in the mission field" only with great diffidence. The
phrase had lost its earlier force. "The whole world is the mission field,
and there is no Church that is not a Church in the mission field."[19] For
Mennonites, still in the first phase of learning how to conduct missions
and with only a few fledgling churches in Asia and Africa, it was
existentially difficult to identify with the emerging internationalist
perspective that would undergird the ecumenical movement.

As already noted, Guy Hershberger believed that in this period
Mennonites were engaged in the recovery of "the Anabaptist vision of
mission and service." Indeed, they did become active in organizing and
conducting missions at home and abroad. But conceptually and
theologically this undertaking was heavily dependent on the larger
Protestant movement. Nowhere is this more evident than with regard to
how the gospel itself was understood. Throughout the nineteenth century,
the Protestant mission movement maintained a "whole gospel" emphasis
based on the dominant themes of evangelical Protestantism. Except for
the absence of the peace ethic, Mennonites found this formulation
generally acceptable. With the rise of the social gospel, on the one hand,
and fundamentalism, on the other, this consensus was severely tested.
Mennonites were not spared this trial.

1918–1970: INTERNATIONALIZATION

This period opened in the aftermath of World War I, with attempts by the
victorious Allied Powers to create a League of Nations for the purpose of

---

[17] See J. S. Shoemaker and J. S. Hartzler, *Among Missions in the Orient and
Observations by the Way* (Scottdale, Pa.: Mennonite Publishing House, 1912),
for an account of the Edinburgh conference.

[18] World Missionary Conference, *The Church in the Mission Field. Report of
Commission II* (Edinburgh: Oliphant, Anderson & Ferrier, 1910).

[19] Ibid., 4. The report goes on to say: "The Commission has perforce accepted
the popular but inexact usage of calling only those regions 'the mission field'
where the Church has become more recently planted, and where its history falls
roughly within the last two centuries."

responding to international conflict through a permanent council and secretariat. The league was based on a covenant that provided for collective security, arbitration of international disputes, reduction of armaments, and open diplomacy. It was a grand and idealistic vision of internationalism, but it soon foundered on the shoals of resurgent nationalism and isolationism. Out of this short-lived experiment only the Permanent Court of International Justice survived.

World War 2 underscored the urgency of finding ways of moderating and resolving conflicts between nations. After the war, a series of new institutions emerged at the initiative of the Allies, starting with the United Nations in 1945, the International Monetary Fund, and the World Bank. The Marshall Plan became the symbol of constructive internationalism. The world economy experienced unprecedented economic growth between 1945 and 1970.

The division of the world into the communist and capitalist blocs, however, quickly compromised this new and vigorous internationalism. Internationalism was soon viewed with cynicism, as a tool for the United States and the Soviet Union to maintain hegemony through their blocs. The emergence of the Nonaligned Movement out of the Bandung Conference in 1955 was the first signal that this bipolar world would prove unruly. By 1970 virtually all independence movements in colonies of the powers had succeeded in winning their political independence.

This preoccupation with liberation from the foreign yoke affected the churches and missions as well. A parallel independence movement took place among mission-founded churches in Asia, Africa, and Latin America. From the beginning, the modern mission movement had been committed to the ideal of self-responsible churches. Those who had lagged in implementing their policy commitments were now under growing pressure to do so.

The conference at Edinburgh in 1910 nurtured initiatives that eventuated in the ecumenical movement: the Faith and Order Commission was organized in 1920, and the international Missionary Council (IMC) in 1921. During the previous decade John R. Mott, IMC chair, had held a series of conferences in Asia and Africa that resulted in the formation of national Christian councils, the infrastructure of the future World Council of Churches. The founding of the World Council was delayed until 1948 because of World War 2.

While these unitive efforts pointed in the direction of worldwide cooperation, a strong counter-force was at work. The modernist-fundamentalist conflict disrupted unity in most churches between 1905 and 1930. Mennonites felt the impact of this conflict. Mennonite missions had been one of the major interfaces between the Mennonite churches and other Protestants, and conservative critics were not slow to expose this fact. Mennonite missionaries continued quietly to fraternize with their Protestant colleagues but did not identify with the ecumenical movement.[20] In addition, the world economic crisis in the 1920s and 1930s allowed only modest mission expansion.

The seminal program development for Mennonites during this period was the organization of the Mennonite Central Committee in 1920. World War 1 had exposed the fundamental differences between the Protestant churches and Mennonites over the question of participation in war. The experience of Mennonite conscientious objectors who served in the American Friends Service Committee relief program in France and the Near East following World War 1 had shown them new possibilities for service by which they could express their pacifist convictions. When Mennonites responded to the call in 1920 to respond to famine conditions in Russia, this experience in Europe and the Near East proved foundational.[21] At a time when constituents put pressure on Mennonite missions to withdraw from association with other Christians, these constituents generally tolerated cooperation by the inter-Mennonite MCC with other agencies in relief programs.

For the missions and their related churches in other countries, this retreat from wider engagement was checked at two points. Soon after the founding of the National Association of Evangelicals in 1943 and the Evangelical Foreign Missions Association in 1945, a number of Mennonite and Brethren in Christ bodies affiliated with these evangelical organizations. This drew them firmly into the evangelical orbit, which was poised for rapid growth during the next several decades. This tendency to withdraw was also rejected by many of the developing churches in Asia, Africa, and Latin America. Typically they were small churches in societies where the total Christian population was a small minority. These communities were far less conscious of denominational differences and felt the importance of solidarity with fellow Christians of whatever persuasion. The channels of relationship varied. In Tanzania, the East African Revival became a primary vehicle for inter-

---

[20] Orie O. Miller, executive secretary of Mennonite Central Committee and Eastern Mennonite Board of Missions and Charities, attended international Missionary Council assemblies on his own.

[21] Hershberger, "Historical Background," gives the context.

denominational fellowship. In Indonesia, the Mennonite churches played their full role in the Council of Churches. In other instances, cooperative theological education programs became the focus for cooperation.

Throughout this period Mennonites produced no substantial works on the theology, history, or practice of Christian mission and service. The recovery of the Anabaptist vision focused largely on questions of Mennonite identity. The groundbreaking work of Guy F. Hershberger, H. A. Fast, and others, with regard to war, the gospel, and the way of peace had no counterpart in regard to the mission of the church to the world.[22] Mennonites continued to depend on evangelical and ecumenical theological and missiological thought.

SINCE 1970: GLOBALIZATION

By the late 1960s, the post–World War 2 economic boom had come to an end. In the 1970s, the bipolar world created in response to the antagonism between the communist and western blocs was beginning to come apart. The notion of the nation state itself was being questioned. Internationalism was based on the premise that the nation state remained the basic unit of economic and political life, but the emerging global reality was driven by economic forces beyond the control of individual nations.[23]

The term "global" entered our vocabulary only in the 1960s, as substitute for "international." During the 1960s, one American Protestant mission board was renamed "Global Program Agency." In popular parlance, "global" remains a synonym for "international," that is, encompassing the whole world. As a technical term, "globalization" is of even more recent coinage and has arisen out of world systems thinking associated particularly with Immanuel Wallerstein[24] and Roland Robertson.[25]

---

[22] This observation is most easily verified by scrutinizing the "Bibliography of Mennonite Missions," *Mission Focus* 12 (December 1984): 49–71.

[23] See Robert B. Reich, *The Work of Nations: Preparing Ourselves for 21st Century Capitalism* (New York: Vintage Books, 1992).

[24] Immanuel Wallerstein, *The Modern World System: Capitalist Agriculture and the Origins of the European World-Economy in the Sixteenth Century* (New York: Academic Press, 1974).

[25] Roland Robertson, *Globalization: Social Theory and Global Culture* (Newberry Park, Calif.: Sage, 1992). Robertson's work on globalization began in the l960s.

Robertson defines the term as follows: "Globalization as a concept refers both to the compression of the world and the intensification of consciousness of the world as a whole."[26] The world has been increasingly compressed and held together by the vast techno-economic and communication networks that have rapidly developed over the past several centuries. According to Robertson, this global system which leads to "the intensification of consciousness" consists of four components: the individual, humankind, nation states, and the world system. Each of the four elements perforce exists in direct relationship with the other three. Change in one element is radiated to the other three, although with vastly differing degrees of impact. These elements are interdependent but in tension with each other. Instability and volatility characterize the system. It never achieves a steady state.

The language of globalization points to a qualitatively new stage in cultural development. Whereas in the past each imperium imposed its particular culture on the empire, recently the world has entered the new phase of globalization. Peter Beyer has argued that the present situation means "the creation of a new global culture with its attendant social structures, one which increasingly becomes the broader social context of *all* particular cultures in the world including those of the West."[27] Global culture is increasingly the arbiter in human development. The particular, whether cultural or religious, is constantly being relativized by the global. However, the global itself is continually being undermined and eroded by competing powers.

The most important conceptual development in mission theory in the past twenty-five years is the notion of "contextuality," introduced in 1972 by Shoki Coe of the Theological Education Fund. For the previous century, the key idea had been "indigeneity." This indicated a process by which something exogenous was introduced and adapted so that it took root in the soil of that culture. Now authority was shifted from the outside agent—be that missionary or service worker—to the local. At the same time, however, it was increasingly evident that ecclesial reality had changed. No local church, regardless of its location, was self-sufficient. What was needed was a new conceptualization of church that recognized the integrity of the local church, but always in relation to the church universal.

---

[26] Ibid., 8.

[27] Peter Beyer, *Religion and Globalization* (Thousand Oaks, Calif.: Sage Publications, 1994), 9.

Mennonites and Brethren in Christ were fully aware of their changing relationships, as a result of nearly a century of international church development. Already by 1970 some conferences in Asia or Africa were larger than the North American body to which they related. This posed a new agenda. How do we achieve the promise of "the new humanity" which embodies the rich variety of peoples from all parts of the world? What new structures will be required to enable this new reality to witness and serve together? The Mennonite World Conference was seen as one means by which this universality might be expressed. But from the outset it was agreed that MWC should not attempt to be more than a mechanism for fostering fellowship through periodic assemblies.[28] MWC did sponsor a series of international consultations— in San Juan, Puerto Rico, in 1975; Hesston, Kansas, in 1978; and Strasbourg, France, in 1984—where the changing Mennonite and Brethren in Christ relationships were studied. In addition, between 1970 and 1994 a series of discussions took place in the Council of Mission Board Secretaries and its successor Council of International Ministries conceding the implications of internationalization and globalization for future relationships and witness.[29] Denominational groups such as the Mennonite Brethren and Brethren in Christ have also worked at internationalizing their program structures.

CONCLUSION

1880–1980 was the Mennonites' "Great Century," because it marked a wholesale redefinition of their identity. Mennonite and Brethren in Christ mission and service ministries have indeed been instruments in creating this global reality. The pioneers a century ago could not have anticipated the scope and scale of change.

The new phenomenon of globalization defines the world today. It contributes to fragmentation and alienation. It leads to the concentration of immense power in the hands of a small group of corporations that

---

[28] Cornelius J. Dyck, "The History of the Mennonite World Conference," in *Mennonite World Handbook: A Survey of Mennonite and Brethren in Christ Churches,* ed. Paul N. Kraybill (Lombard, Ill.: Mennonite World Conference, 1978), 1–9. This purpose was reaffirmed in a resolution at the Curitiba assembly in 1972.

[29] Four summary statements from these consultations are appendices to Wilbert R. Shenk, *God's New Economy: Interdependence and Mission* (Elkhart, Ind.: Mission Focus, 1988).

operate beyond national boundaries and conventional political constraints.

The original globalization was the reign of God enacted in the first coming of Jesus the Messiah, and continually reenacted through the community of disciples that obeys the call to follow him. The goal of the reign of God is to unite all things in Jesus Christ (Eph. 1:10; Col. 1:20), the essence of the mission of Jesus (Matt. 4:17; Mark 1:15). Other globalization efforts are based on human striving and power-mongering. What sets Christian mission and service apart from other human initiatives—especially the myth of redemptive violence which is foundational to the global world system—is that Christian mission witnesses to the reign of God that arises out of self-sacrificing love. Christians cannot escape this new globalization. As disciples, we are called to exercise discernment with respect to all powers and movements that do not submit to the lordship of Jesus Christ.

There is no doubt that Mennonite mission and service efforts have been used to extend the reign of God around the world in response to the original globalization. These have been the fruit of messianic renewal among the Mennonite peoplehood. The most tangible evidence of this are the hundreds of local congregations scattered around the world where the God of Jesus the Messiah is worshiped and obeyed. This is the basic criterion by which we must judge and evaluate whether we have been faithful: faith in Jesus the Messiah reproduced in the lives of others.

In 1970 Guy Hershberger concluded that Mennonite mission efforts were "approaching maturity." However, he did not tell us what this meant. What is maturity in mission? Is it possible to achieve such a state? Is it even a proper or desirable goal? Repeatedly, we observe that history is a poor teacher. So-called "lessons from history" are not readily accepted by the next generation. Indeed, the continually changing historical context requires fresh wrestling with truth and obedience in light of new demands. I suggest there are six developments of the past century of engagement in mission and service that can contribute to the maturing process to which Hershberger alluded:

*1. Mennonites have developed an enlarged and enriched understanding of the gospel as God's word that embraces the whole of human need.* We are confronted with various "gospels," which undergird ideologies or interests, including efforts that pit word against deed. These instrumental uses of the gospel result in distortion. There are not multiple gospels, only our reductionist versions. Reductionisms weaken and denature. Maturity requires a readiness to embrace the gospel in its fullness. To reiterate: the gospel is as wide and comprehensive as human need.

2. *Mennonites have acquired a deepened conviction and confidence in the gospel, as a result of participating in its continuing spread to peoples who heretofore had not heard and embraced the gospel of Jesus the Messiah.* This experience has reconfirmed that the gospel is indeed "the power of God" to create "one new humanity" out of disparate parts; that erstwhile enemies can be reconciled through the atoning work of Jesus Christ; and that the gospel is the source of healing and hope.

3. *Mennonites have come to a recognition that agencies, methods, and strategies are only instruments and should never be regarded as otherwise.* Maturity means the readiness to subject our methods and means to honest scrutiny in light of experience and growth.

4. *Mennonites have experienced programmatic innovation in the twentieth century, spurred by their opposition to war.* World War 1 provided a testing ground for the Historic Peace Churches. By force of circumstance they were driven to "discover" service as a way of expressing their refusal to participate in warfare. As World War 2 approached, the churches worked out a large-scale program for their members who refused to participate in military service but were ready to engage in an alternative through the Civilian Public Service program. As has been widely noted, CPS was seminal. It spawned a range of service ministries and gave legitimacy to a theology of peacemaking.

5. *Perhaps as a result of historical circumstances, Mennonite theologies of peace have been developed independent of mission.* In response to the challenge of external forces, work on theology of peace began earlier and has been the main focus for the most creative and distinctive contribution of Mennonites and Brethren in Christ in theology and ethics. In contrast, their contributions to a theology of mission have been largely confined to the period since 1970.[30] This, then, is a challenge to continue working at the unfinished task of an integrated theology of mission that can undergird the whole mission of the church.

6. *The Anabaptists correctly focused on the nature of the church as the critical question of the sixteenth century; evidence suggests that this is a critical question for twenty-first-century Mennonites as well.* Mennonites and Brethren in Christ are tempted to confuse the ethnic-

---

[30] See chapter 6 of this book.

based community for the community that arises in response to the reign of God. Treating the former as the sine qua non of *ecclesia* is a betrayal of the gospel and the Anabaptist heritage; in the latter lies the promise of God's salvation (Acts 15). The former is merely self-serving; the latter is God's instrument of the *missio Dei*. The quest for God's community of shalom must continue. But the context for this search is vastly different from what it was even a century ago. This search for the meaning of church in the twenty-first century is taking place in a global context. Local reality must constantly be juxtaposed with the global mission of God's people. To work out the nature and mission of the church effectively in this changing world will require courage and imagination. But it is the most promising prospect conceivable.

The globalization of the Mennonite and Brethren in Christ community over the past century urges us on toward maturity by challenging the ever-present temptation to turn inward. It is a signal from God that our missional responsibility to the world is not yet fulfilled.

# 4

## *Growth through Mission*

This chapter is an exploration of the ebb and flow in the development of the Brethren in Christ and Mennonite churches over the course of the past 150 years, in response to the mission impulse. Such an investigation could be carried out in a variety of ways. In order to keep the study focused, we will ask essentially one question: how many new cross-cultural missions were established during each decade since 1850 by Mennonite and Brethren in Christ mission agencies for the purpose of developing new churches? This method can, of course, be criticized for its narrow focus. It does not call for qualitative evaluation. Nonetheless, it allows us to observe a crucial dimension of mission—the action by which the physical presence of the church is extended and established in new places. This physical presence becomes the basis for a range of further developments, including new mission initiative. The character and scope of the Mennonite family have changed vastly in a century and a half. The overview presented here should help us to apprehend the framework within which the writing of history and the continuing development of theology must be set in the future.

NINETEENTH-CENTURY BEGINNINGS

Until the nineteenth century, the main stimulus for movement among Mennonites was migration, typically triggered by religious persecution or the search for economic opportunity. Migration in response to religious intolerance or persecution remains a continuing theme in the Mennonite saga until late in the twentieth century. But, as described in the previous two chapters, in the nineteenth century a new source of change was introduced, namely, growth through mission. Dutch Mennonites set this precedent.[1]

---

Reprinted, with revisions, by permission of Mennonite World Conference, from *Mennonite World Handbook,* ed. Paul N. Kraybill (Lombard, Ill.: Mennonite World Conference 1978), 20–31.

[1] Alle Hoekema, "Why the Dutch Were the First Mennonites to Send Missionaries Overseas," *Conrad Grebel Review* 15, no. 1/2 (winter/spring 1997): 23–34.

Dutch Mennonite relations with English Baptists extend back to the first decades of the seventeenth century, when Baptists fled to the Netherlands to escape religious persecution in Great Britain. The Baptists organized their missionary society in 1792, and the next year sent William Carey and his family to India. This pioneering mission soon attracted widespread attention. Dutch Mennonites followed this development with interest, and individuals began contributing financial support to the Baptist mission at Serampore. In 1821 the Baptist Missionary Society authorized the formation of a Dutch committee. The officers and most members were Mennonites.

By 1847 the Dutch Mennonites decided they needed their own society in order to carry on missionary work in the Dutch Indies. They organized the Dutch Mennonite Mission Association (Doopsgezinde Mission Zendings Vereeniging). In 1851 this association commissioned Pieter Jansz (1820–1904) as their first missionary to the Dutch East Indies.[2] He selected an area in north-central Java and began laying the foundation of what became the Indonesian Mennonite churches. Like William Carey and his associates in India, an important part of Jansz's missionary career was his work as a Bible translator.

Evangelical Pietist influence reached the Russian Mennonites in the nineteenth century, helping to revitalize an ebbing church and community life. Occasionally Swiss and German missionaries did deputation among the Mennonites in Russia. Because Russian law forbade groups such as the Mennonites to evangelize beyond their own communities, the chief outlets for this growing interest were to extend renewal within the Mennonite communities and to support foreign missions. In 1854 the Russian Mennonites joined their German and Swiss brothers and sisters in supporting the work of the Dutch association. In 1871 Heinrich Dirks (1842–1915) from Russia founded a mission on Sumatra under the Dutch association. Nine couples and ten single missionaries followed Dirks in service on Sumatra and Java. Indeed, after 1878 the Russian and German churches provided all new missionaries sent to Java and Sumatra. Only Russian Mennonites staffed the mission in Sumatra from its founding in 1871 until it was handed over to the German Lutherans in 1928.

In spite of such progress, some Russian Mennonites wanted more radical change. This group formed the Mennonite Brethren Church in

---

[2] Alle G. Hoekema, "Peter Jansz (1820–1904)—First Mennonite Missionary to Java," *Mennonite Quarterly Review* 52 (January 1978): 58–76.

1860. They emphasized evangelism and missionary outreach. Risking arrest, some Mennonite Brethren evangelized their Russian neighbors. Gerhard Wieler was imprisoned in 1865 for baptizing converts of Orthodox background.

Because of their close relationship with the German Baptists, the Mennonite Brethren channeled much of their missionary support through the Baptist Missionary Society. Several MB members joined the Baptist Mission in Cameroon, West Africa, and in 1890 Abram and Mary Friesen took an assignment with the Baptist Mission at Nalgonda, near Hyderabad, India.

The Wesleyan revival movement in the eighteenth century touched North American Mennonites. The Brethren in Christ emerged out of this cross-fertilization. The eighteenth-century revival changed the individual and introduced new earnestness in congregational life. However, it did not include a vision for world mission.

In the late nineteenth century, the Moody-Sankey revivals and growing contact with Protestant missions helped breach Mennonite cultural isolation. While Mennonites and Brethren in Christ attempted to maintain the uniqueness of their heritage, they also began to acknowledge their responsibility to the world. Mennonites in North America shared in the great migration westward. Many of these people became scattered across the continent in small isolated communities without adequate spiritual leadership. The needs of these frontier settlements provided early impetus to "home missions."

European immigrants brought with them to North America reports of the work being done by the Dutch association and other mission societies. Interested individuals such as Daniel Hoch (1806–78) of Ontario began to promote missions in the 1850s, and helped to organize a mission society in 1859. Two Mennonite congregations in Iowa convened a conference in 1859 to promote a united missionary witness.

Most North American Mennonite and Brethren in Christ groups in the nineteenth century were only loosely organized. Mission committees and boards exerted little influence or leadership. Influential individuals provided the main initiative. Eusebius Hershey (1823–91) was one such North American Mennonite to go to another continent as a missionary. He sailed for Africa in 1890 without official support. Hershey died in Sierra Leone in 1891, some six months after he arrived.

Hershey was not the first North American who volunteered for cross-cultural missionary service, however. Samuel S. Haury (1847–1929), a General Conference Mennonite, offered himself for assignment under the Dutch association in Indonesia. When these plans failed to materialize, his church sent him to establish a mission in the Arapaho Indian Territory (now Oklahoma) in 1880. The General Conference Mennonites subsequently established missions among the Cheyenne in Montana and the Hopi in Arizona. The North American Mennonite Brethren established a mission to the Comanche in Oklahoma in 1894.

Already in their 1879 annual conference, the Mennonite Brethren adopted a resolution calling for their congregations to take weekly offerings for missions. They elected a missions committee to administer these funds and appointed an itinerant evangelist to stir up interest among the congregations. During the first years, the Mennonite Brethren used their money to support the Baptist Mission in Andra Pradesh, India. In 1898 they decided they would sponsor their own missionary work rather than rely on other churches.

George Lambert (1853–1928), Mennonite layman from Elkhart, Indiana, visited India in 1894–95. When famine struck India in 1896–97, world attention focused on this great disaster.[3] With his natural talent as a publicist and promoter, Lambert visited many congregations, appealing for relief funds. Then in 1897 Lambert went to India to supervise distribution of food supplies. David Goerz undertook a similar program of distribution in India in 1899.

The Mennonite Church appealed for missionaries to go to India in 1897. In 1898 three candidates were appointed. They arrived in India in March 1899, and settled in the Dhamtari, Madhya Pradesh, area. The North American Mennonite Brethren also sent four missionaries to India in 1899 to join their Russian MB colleagues in the Hyderabad region.

Two other overseas missions were founded before the turn of the century. The Brethren in Christ sent their first missionaries abroad in 1898 to Southern Rhodesia. And two members of the Mennonite Brethren in Christ (later the Missionary Church) entered Turkey that same year. They worked with an interdenominational agency that served children orphaned as a result of the 1896 massacre of Armenians. This work was closed in 1914.

---

[3] George Lambert, *Around the Globe and through Bible Lands: Notes and Observations on the Various Countries through Which the Writer Traveled* (Elkhart, Ind.: Mennonite Publishing Company, 1896); and George Lambert, *India, the Horror-Stricken Empire: Containing a Full Account of the Famine, Plague, and Earthquake of 1896–7; Including a Complete Narrative of the Relief Work through the Home and Foreign Commission* (Elkhart, Ind.: Mennonite Publishing Company, 1898).

1900–1909

Mennonite support for missions grew stronger during the next decade. The General Conference Mennonites commissioned two missionary families to establish a mission in India. They arrived in India in December 1900 and located at Champa, Madhya Pradesh.

The following year, H. C. and Nellie (Schmidt) Bartel went to China with the Horace Houlding Mission. Members of the Krimmer Mennonite Brethren, the Bartels drew support from the KMB and MB constituencies. They worked first in southern Chihli province. Four years later, they relocated to neighboring Shantung province. In 1912 the KMB, MB, Evangelical Mennonite Brethren, and Missionary Church Association reorganized the Bartel mission as the China Mennonite Mission Society. This mission thus became one of the earliest ventures in inter-Mennonite cooperation.

The Evangelical Mennonite Brethren entered into an arrangement with the Mennonite Board of Missions to send workers to India under MBM auspices. They commissioned P. A. and Helena Friesen for service in India in 1907. This arrangement was abandoned some years later, and the Friesens affiliated with the Mennonite Church in 1916.

The Mennonite Brethren in Christ formed their missionary society with a view to working in West Africa. They sent missionaries to Nigeria in 1905.

From their base in Southern Rhodesia, the Brethren in Christ extended their work to Zambia in 1906.[4] Some members of the Mennonite Brethren in Christ began work in West Bengal, India, in 1908. Later this mission was placed under direction of the Missionary society.

H. J. and Maria (Miller) Brown, General Conference Mennonites, arrived in China in 1909 and two years later established a mission at Hopeh. The General Conference Mennonite Foreign Mission Board assumed responsibility for this mission in 1914.

One of the themes running through the history of these formative years is the degree to which the initiative rested with interested and concerned members rather than with the churches, mission committees, and boards. Instead of acting boldly and providing leadership, mission boards moved cautiously. When they were convinced these lay ventures

---

[4] H. Frank Kipe, "From Mission to Church: Zambia and Zimbabwe," in *Brethren in Christ History and Life* 17 (August 1994): 145–56.

enjoyed constituency support, they would get behind them with official sponsorship and oversight. But quite a few Mennonite and Brethren in Christ constituents simply joined other missionary societies, both denominational and nondenominational, that were already well established and could offer attractive opportunities. One result of this situation was that many of these people eventually severed their ties to the Mennonite constituency altogether.

The missionary spirit that had been stirring Mennonites on both sides of the Atlantic during the nineteenth century was one dimension of a larger renewal movement. Mennonites entered the task of world mission as latecomers, hardly daring to formulate a distinctive approach to mission. In North America the emergence of educational institutions ran parallel to the formation of mission agencies. Educational leaders often were also active in the promotion of missions. Advocates of higher education justified it in terms of training young people for world mission. It was taken for granted that mission work required the founding of schools of various kinds. Only properly qualified teachers could do this work. Strangely enough, medical missions had failed to win a regular place in mission work until late in the nineteenth century. The Dutch Mennonite Mission started schools on Java almost from the beginning, but medical work was added only after 1900. Even then the medical program on Java was funded by government, rather than by the mission.

## 1910–1919

The Student Volunteer Movement gave major impetus to world mission from the late 1880s onward. John R. Mott challenged students with the slogan: "The Evangelization of the World in This Generation." Students in Mennonite colleges and academies were stirred by this appeal.

In 1910 the landmark World Missionary Conference met at Edinburgh, Scotland. Three Mennonites attended: J. S. Shoemaker, (secretary of Mennonite Board of Missions), J. S. Hartzler (president of Mennonite Board of Missions), and Alfred Wiebe (missionary candidate with the General Conference mission board). One of the high moments of Edinburgh 1910 came when V. S. Azariah of India called for a new basis for relationship between West and East. He concluded with these provocative words, as recorded in the World Missionary Conference report: "You have given your goods to feed the poor. You have given your bodies to be burned. We also ask for love. Give us *friends!*"[5]

The Mennonite Board of Missions Personnel Manual (1898) defined the aim of missions to be "the raising up of self-supporting and self-extending churches.... Native helpers especially should be afforded all possible help and encouragement; as they become able, they should be allowed to bear responsibility and the element of foreign teaching, pastoral care, and supervision be gradually withdrawn."[6] This was the standard theory of mission on which the modern missionary movement was based.

Hartzler and Shoemaker went from Edinburgh to India, carrying the challenge of Edinburgh with them. While in India in 1911 Hartzler and Shoemaker helped the missionaries conclude several years of discussion with the decision to organize a church conference. The first Mennonite conference to emerge out of a mission was thus organized in January 1912 as the Mennonite Church in India.

In 1914 the Mennonite Brethren founded the Telegu Convention. The first annual convention met in April 1916. The convention was designed to unite and strengthen the Telegu church, develop Indian leadership, and promote growth of the church. Missionaries were allowed to be only advisory members of the convention.

Four new Mennonite missions were formed in this decade. L. B. and Rose (Boehning) Haigh sailed for Congo in 1911, sponsored by the Defenseless Mennonites and Central Conference Mennonites. Soon several other Mennonite groups joined the first two in sponsoring the second inter-Mennonite mission agency. This one became the Congo Inland Mission.

That same year, F. J. and Agnes (Harder) Wiens, Mennonite Brethren, went to China. In 1919 the Mennonite Brethren Board of Foreign Missions adopted the Wienses' work in South China.

In 1912 A. A. Jensen left for Zaire and founded a mission related to the Mennonite Brethren. The Mennonite Brethren conference did not give official recognition to this mission until 1939.

The Mennonite Board of Missions sent J. W. Shank on a six-month trip to South America in 1911. Shank returned, urging the board to send

---

[5] World Missionary Conference, *The History and Records of the Conference* (Edinburgh and London: Oliphant, Anderson, and Ferrier, 1910), 9:315.

[6] Personnel Manual, Mennonite Board of Missions and Charities (Elkhart, Ind., 1898).

a mission to Argentina. Fearing insufficient church support, the board delayed sending the first two missionary couples until 1917.

In 1913 the Brethren in Christ established a mission in the rural Saharsa District, 200 miles from Calcutta in northern Bihar Province, India.[7]

World War 1 dominated this decade, disrupting the world politically and economically. In the aftermath of World War 1, relief and rehabilitation programs in Europe and the Middle East laid the basis for later specialized relief and development programs. Mennonite conscientious objectors to war joined the Committee for Armenian and Syrian Relief to help Middle Eastern refugees, while others worked with the American Friends Service Committee reconstruction program in France. More than eighty young Mennonites served with these and other agencies.

Traditionally missions incorporated various services as a part of their work. If an emergency arose, they gave relief assistance. They built schools, hospitals, clinics, and promoted agricultural and economic development. The World War 1 experience stimulated the development of specialist services to refugees and war sufferers. Mennonites shared in the growing complexity of mission and service agencies. They did not always maintain a clear theological basis for what they were doing. During this period the modernists debated with the fundamentalists about the content to the gospel and the extent of Christian responsibility. Rather than clarifying the issues, the debate had polarizing effect. Most Mennonites continued to believe that the gospel was to be proclaimed as well as demonstrated through compassionate service, but they imbibed a theology that supported a dichotomy between the Word proclaimed and the Word demonstrated, with proclamation given priority over demonstration.

## 1920–1929

The 1920s was a time of slow overseas mission expansion. Only one new mission was sent during this entire decade. The Krimmer Mennonite Brethren sent Frank V. and Agnes (Ebel) Wiebe to Mongolia in 1921. The Wiebes reached China in 1922 and spent a year with the China Mennonite Mission Society before proceeding to Mongolia.

---

[7] Harvey R. Sider, "From Mission to Church: India," *Brethren in Christ History and Life* 17 (August 1994): 113–44.

While the rate of founding new missions was nearly at a standstill, existing missions were consolidated and expanded. The Mennonite Brethren in Christ reorganized their work as the United Missionary Society and assumed responsibility for the work started in India some fifteen years before. Other boards underwent similar strengthening of constituency support. In India the Mennonite Brethren Telegu Convention formed its own home mission and took responsibility for the Kalva–Kurthy field. The Indian church commissioned and supported three missionaries for this work.

The Sumatra mission in Indonesia, however, had to be dissolved in 1928. This mission had been staffed and supported financially largely by Russian Mennonites working through the Dutch Mission Association. Soon after the Bolsheviks came to power in Russia in 1917, it became impossible for Mennonites in Russia to maintain missionary interest abroad. When the last Mennonite missionary to serve in Sumatra, Peter Nachtigal, died, the Lutherans in the area assumed responsibility. A small group of Sumatrans refused to accept this development and continued to consider themselves Mennonites.

During this decade two developments dominated Mennonite missionary experience. In the aftermath of the Bolshevik takeover, Russia faced confusion and political instability. To this were added famine and severe economic hardship. In response to the desperate situation of Mennonites in Russia, North American Mennonites organized the Mennonite Central Committee in 1920, as an inter-Mennonite agency to take assistance to Russia. Emergency relief led next to assistance to refugees who wished to be resettled in North and South America. North American Mennonites contributed $2.5 million in relief programs during the ten years following World War 1, and dozens of Mennonite young people saw the world through new eyes as they gave themselves in relief service.

The second development involved the international political order. Already in the latter part of the nineteenth century, peoples in lands colonized by the European powers began organizing movements to gain their political independence. By the 1920s Chinese, Indian, and Indonesian nationalists openly challenged their colonial governments. The governments struck back, quelling riots and jailing leaders. Churches and missions faced similar pressures. The emerging churches wanted to be freed from mission control. Both missionaries and indigenous Christians expended much energy in trying to understand and come to terms with the new day.

The decade closed with the world economic system in deep crisis following the collapse of the capital markets in 1929.

## 1930–1939

For the next ten years, missions operated under great financial constraints. Missionary candidates received rejection slips rather than appointments, as mission boards worked their way out of financial difficulties.

Mennonites emigrated from Canada to Paraguay in 1927–28, and refugees from Russia joined them beginning in 1930. In 1932 these Mennonite colonists organized a mission, Licht den Indianern, in order to evangelize among the Indians of the Chaco. A year later the Church of God in Christ, Mennonite (Holdeman) sent their first missionaries to Mexico.

In 1934 the Lancaster (Pennsylvania) Conference of the Mennonite Church appointed its first four missionaries to East Africa. They entered Tanzania determined to capitalize on the fruits of missionary experience elsewhere. Aware of the need to respect indigenous peoples, Eastern Board missionaries sought to bring the new church to self-responsibility as early as possible.

The missionary witness in Paraguay expanded when the Mennonite Brethren established a mission to the Indians of the Chaco in 1935. Eventually Licht den Indianern also came under MB board control.

This decade closed with the world in a new state of heightened tension. The Nazis were in power in Germany and preparing to invade other nations. War was imminent both in Europe and Asia. On the eve of World War 2, Mennonites were at work on three continents where 90 years before they had not set foot—Asia, Africa, and Latin America. The Mennonite world had become much larger through participation in mission and service programs.

## 1940–1949

Anticipating the disruption war would bring, the Dutch mission completed organization of the Javanese church in 1940. Less than two years later the Japanese invaded Indonesia and interned all missionaries. The whole world felt the impact of World War 2, but the areas most directly affected were Europe, the Middle East, and Asia. Missionaries could not go on furlough, and mission boards could not send out new workers. Churches in war-affected areas often faced restrictions on their common life.

Mennonites and Brethren in Christ in North America joined forces through the Mennonite Central Committee to bring emergency relief to Europe, the Middle East, and China. It soon became apparent that help was needed in other areas, such as India. By the end of the decade, the MCC constituency had contributed $12 million in cash and commodities for emergency relief, and some 700 volunteers had served around the world.

The embargo on sending missionaries was temporary. MBM started a new mission in India already in 1940 by re-deploying four missionaries from Madhya Pradesh to Bihar. They followed the same pattern again in 1943 by relocating missionaries from Central Argentina to the Argentine Chaco.

When the war ended, mission board treasuries showed surpluses, and missionary candidates began coming forward. Already in 1945 five new missions were launched: the General Conference Mennonites and the Mennonite Brethren both entered Colombia; the Mennonite Church Association began work in Dominican Republic, Ecuador, and Sierra Leone; and MBM sent workers to Puerto Rico. In 1946 the Evangelical Mennonite Church (U.S.) sent a mission to Dominican Republic, and the following year MBM commissioned six missionaries for West China. In 1948 the Mennonite Relief and Service Committee began a service program in Ethiopia for which, subsequently, the Eastern Mennonite Board of Missions assumed responsibility. Dutch, German, Swiss, and French Mennonites formed the European Mennonite Evangelization Committee to carry forward their work.

The MCA entered Jamaica in 1949. That same year Virginia Mennonites, in cooperation with MBM, began working in Sicily. MBM also sent its first two missionary couples to Japan in 1949. The Dutch Mennonites appointed missionaries to Irian Jaya in a joint venture with other Dutch missionary societies.

World War 2 marks a watershed for the missionary movement. The war had scarcely ended when Indonesian nationalists declared their independence from the Dutch, and the Indians entered into the final phase of their emancipation from British rule. Even more momentous was the communist takeover in China. Whether these newly independent nations like India and Indonesia continued to tolerate the presence of Christian missionaries, or whether as in the case of China they expelled foreigners, a new political and social climate had been established. The adjustments in mission-church relations begun in the 1920s now had to be completed. The Indonesian Mennonites offer one illustration. During

World War 2 and the war of revolution, the church and mission had been forcibly separated by political and military circumstances. After the Dutch government recognized Indonesia's independence in 1949, the Indonesian church invited the European and North American Mennonites to join them in rebuilding their church.

China was different. Mennonite missions and churches in China experienced the full impact of Mao Tse-tung's rise to power. Between 1948 and 1951 all missionaries, with one exception, had to leave the country. Loyal Bartel, son of the founder of the China Mennonite Mission Society, elected to remain. He died in China in 1971. With the closing of China, virtually all contact with some 7,000 members of Chinese Mennonite churches was lost.

## 1950–1959

Although Mennonite Central Committee always tried to relate its relief and service programs to local churches, it did not restrict its work to areas where Mennonite and Brethren in Christ missions were located. MCC's rapid expansion worldwide in the 1950s was more than matched by the mission boards. Rarely was this expansion coordinated, because a division of labor was assumed: relief and service programs responded to emergency human needs, and the missions were dedicated to long-term church development.

In 1950 the Mennonite Brethren went to Japan, General Conference Mennonites to Mexico, MBM to Belgium, Conservative Mennonite Board of Missions to Germany, and EMM to Honduras. The following year the General Conference Mennonites sent their first missionaries to Japan. During this time the French Mennonite Missions Committee became active in the Chad as a member of the interdenominational Sudan United Mission.

The MCA entered Haiti in 1952, and MBM initiated missions to Alaska and England. In 1953 the Mennonite Brethren began working in Austria and Germany, the Brethren in Christ started work in Japan, EMM opened work in Somalia and northeastern France and joined with MBM in sponsoring a mission in Israel. MBM also established a mission in a Paris suburb that year.

In 1954 the General Conference Mennonites took over responsibility for the program MCC had operated on Taiwan since 1948. The Evangelical Mennonite Conference of Canada undertook their first venture in mission by sending workers to Mexico in 1954. MBM began working in South Brazil and Uruguay that same year, while the

Franconia (Pennsylvania) Mennonite Conference of the Mennonite Church dispatched missionaries to Cuba, as did the Brethren in Christ.

The Virginia Conference of the Mennonite Church expanded its work overseas by sending missionaries to Jamaica in 1955, and the Missionary Church Association and MBM started new missions in Brazil. In 1956 the General Conference Mennonites became involved in Uruguay, and MBM entered Ghana. The following year MBM established work in Algeria, and EMM entered Germany, Luxembourg, and Vietnam.

The Franconia Mennonite Conference sent its first missionaries to Mexico in 1958, and the Mennonite Brethren, following up contacts made from Colombia, began a unique missionary effort in Panama. The MB missionaries were in residence only a few months per year. Local believers carried the primary responsibility for Christian witness and church leadership from the beginning.

In the final year of the decade, 1959, Mennonites entered three more fields: EMC (Canada) to Paraguay, the Pacific Mennonite Conference Mission Board (MC) to northwest Mexico, and MBM to Nigeria.

In the 1950s at least 37 new missions were sent out to all parts of the world. Home missions were also expanding during this period. In addition to growth in the number of new missions at home and abroad, existing missions and churches learned increasingly that they were centers of missionary witness and shared this responsibility.

The GC and MB missions in Colombia experienced intense persecution during the years 1948–57, when the government supported Roman Catholic opposition to all Protestants, but the missions managed to continue their work. In 1959 Fidel Castro's communist government came to power in Cuba. The BIC and Franconia Mennonite missions evacuated their missionaries from the country, along with most other expatriates.

In 1958 most of the North American Mennonite and Brethren in Christ mission boards participated in organizing the Council of Mission Board Secretaries (COMBS; after 1976 Council of International Ministries). Mission leaders recognized that with rapid expansion came problems of overlapping, both with other missions and with MCC as the relief and development agency for all Mennonites. The MCC was broadening the scope of its work to include development, education, and health care. Inevitably this raised questions concerning the philosophy and theology of missions and service which earlier were passed over. Now agency identities were at stake. One of the issues COMBS debated first was the relationship between missions and the peace witness. Should peace be treated as a special vocation to be handled through an agency such as the MCC Peace Section, or was peace integral to the gospel and therefore a responsibility of all missionaries and service workers? Admittedly, Mennonite missions had followed the typical Protestant interpretation of the gospel in their missionary witness, and heretofore the historical Anabaptist-Mennonite understanding of the gospel of peace had played no significant role in missionary thinking and practice.

## 1960–1969

The sense of crisis in the 1950s continued into the new decade. Cries of "Missionary, Go Home!" were heard from several sides. Beginning with Ghana in 1958, the continent of Africa underwent rapid political transformation as one colony after the other became independent. The transition was not always peaceful. Following war against the Belgian colonials, the Congo experienced civil war and unrest for several years, with missions and churches suffering terribly. U.S. President John F. Kennedy declared the 1960s to be the Decade of Development, and international development agencies promoted all kinds of programs. Mission and service agencies joined in a range of development projects. The results were disappointing.

By 1967 the international economy began to slow as the post–World War 2 boom came to an end. The rate of mission expansion slowed and Brethren in Christ and Mennonites started only eleven new missions during these years. Disillusioned by the Vietnam War and the emptiness of materialism, young people were reluctant to commit themselves to Christian mission.

The EMM entered British Honduras (Belize) in 1960. Two years later Rosedale Mennonite Missions began work in Costa Rica. In 1963 the CGCM extended their efforts to Nigeria. As a part of their overall adjustment to the new situation in East Africa, the EMM opened an office in Nairobi, Kenya, in 1965, where they assisted newly established Mennonite churches founded in Kenya by Mennonite immigrants from Tanzania. The Brethren in Christ began a witness in Nicaragua in 1965, and EMM sent workers to Hong Kong that year. Also in 1965 a group from the Muria Christian Church (Gereja-Gereja Kristen Muria Indonesia) founded the Pengutusan Injil dan Pelayanan Kasih

(PIPKA/Board of Missions and Service).[8] Subsequently this board was brought under the GKMI. In 1966 the EMC (Canada) entered Nicaragua and the EMM collaborated with the Washington-Franklin Conference (Pennsylvania/Maryland) of the Mennonite Church in founding a mission in Guatemala. The Virginia Conference sent workers to Guyana in 1969.

By the end of the 1960s Mennonite missions and related churches had experienced the full spectrum of mission-church struggles. Churches established following World War 2 were ready for autonomy and self-responsibility by the 1960s. Increasingly the younger churches asked what their own missionary responsibility should be. The Puerto Rico Conference sent a missionary couple to minister to Spanish migrants in Belgium in 1968. At the same time the Japan Mennonite Church commissioned a couple to Quito, Ecuador, to work with a missionary radio program beamed to the large Japanese emigrant community in Latin America.

## 1970–1979

In 1970 MBM and Mennonite Brethren Board of Missions/Services took official steps to change their historical relationships to their counterpart churches in India. In both cases the boards withdrew missionaries from assignments in direct relationship to the churches. The Indian churches looked for ways of increasing their own efforts in witness and service.

This development brought another issue into sharper focus. No one was interested in simply severing historical ties between the churches that sent the missions and the churches that emerged as a result. How could a worldwide brotherhood discover and develop means for a united missionary witness to the world?

After several years of preparation, the Argentine Mennonite Church, MBM, and the COM entered Bolivia as a three-way partnership. Jose and Soledad Godoy, from Argentina, began their ministry in Bolivia in May 1971. Also in 1971 the Virginia Mennonite Board of Missions entered Trinidad and Tobago. EMM sent a missionary couple to work with a group of churches in the Philippines as teachers and counselors. The nation of Pakistan experienced a civil war in 1971, leading to a division of that country into Pakistan and Bangladesh. The First Asian Mennonite Conference met at Dhamtari, India, in 1972. The conference focused on the missionary task facing the Asian churches. When famine

---

[8]   Charles Christano, "PIPKA: An Indonesian Response to Mission," *International Bulletin of Missionary Research* 6, no. 4 (October 1982): 169–72.

struck Bangladesh in 1973, the Asian Mennonite Conference invited the world brotherhood to participate in a united ministry. The Mennonite Brethren sent the first workers to Bangladesh in 1974, and others followed during the next several years.

The CGCM began work in the Philippines in 1974, and the following year they entered Burkina Faso. The EMC (Canada) sent missionaries to Germany in 1975. The CGCM continued to expand their efforts by entering Dominican Republic and Guatemala in 1976.

In April 1975 the Vietnam War ended, with the North Vietnamese the victors. Mennonites had been working in the country since 1954. Although several Mennonite service workers remained in the country for a year following the change in government, regular visits with the congregation in Ho Chi Minh City (formerly Saigon) were not allowed.

A new departure in 1976 was the invitation extended by PIPKA to the MB Board of Missions/Services to participate with them in leadership training. Eastern Mennonite Missions and Mennonite Central Committee appointed two missionary families to be part of a PIPKA-sponsored team to develop new churches in Kalimantan. From the outset it was agreed that PIPKA was the leader, and all administrative and program decisions were made by the Indonesians. This was a new model of international cooperation.

Also in 1976 two new mission ventures were started in Spain. The Mennonite Brethren sent several missionary couples to the Madrid area. After several years' conversation between members of the Spanish congregation in Brussels and MBM, the latter assigned a missionary couple to a teaching ministry in Spain. Several members of the congregation then returned to Spain and participated in the founding of communities of worship and witness in Barcelona and in Burgos. The AIMM and the Congolese Mennonite Church began studying possible joint missionary work in another African country. This initiative led to the opening of work in Burkina Faso in 1978.

Already in the 1960s several trends emerged that pointed to new patterns that would mark missions for the rest of the century. The western mission agencies increasingly turned to short-term workers to staff programs. Often these short-term missionaries were specialists in medical or educational services. Mennonite agencies also appointed a growing number of their workers to serve with other missions or churches such as African Independent Churches with no expectation that this would add members to Mennonite membership rolls.

## 1980–1989

Viewed in the context of the period 1940–1999, the 1980s was the decade of the fewest new mission initiatives: only five new missions were undertaken. The reasons for this are several.[9] A number of the older Mennonite and Brethren in Christ mission agencies had changes in leadership accompanied by reorganization. Financial support was eroded by inflation, and the number of recruits for missionary service continued to decline. To some extent this was the result of trends in the international economy. But as noted above, the trend toward increased reliance on short-term workers caused a basic shift in the way agencies carried out their programs. The result was a gradual shrinking of program. This is reflected in the following information reported by the five largest Mennonite agencies, taken from the *Mission Handbook.*[10]

| Year | 1979 | | 1986 | | 1989 | | 1993 | | 1999 | |
|---|---|---|---|---|---|---|---|---|---|---|
| Agency | W† | C‡ | W | C | W | C | W | C | W | C |
| COM | 122 | 15 | 122 | 15 | 133 | 15 | 69 | 19 | 44 | 22 |
| EMM | 88 | 18 | 108 | 21 | 81 | 26 | 95 | 21 | 95 | 20 |
| MBM | 125 | 22 | 90 | 26 | 115 | 18 | 81 | 30 | 80 | 19 |
| MBM/S | 158 | 21 | NR | 22 | 126 | 22 | 110 | 15 | 77 | 26 |
| MCC | 431 | 42 | 527 | 48 | 504 | 51 | 424 | 50 | 381 | 52 |

†Workers
‡Countries

The data used in this summary are problematic. The categories for defining workers have continued to change. This is reflected in the fact that the 1993–95 *Mission Handbook*[11] introduced a new way of reporting personnel statistics. "Fully Supported Personnel Overseas" was divided

---

[9] See Wilbert R. Shenk, *Changing Frontiers of Mission* (Maryknoll: Orbis Books, 1999), 166–85, for an analysis of historical and contextual causes of these shifts.

[10] Published periodically by Missions Advanced Research and Communication Center, a division of World Vision.

[11] *Mission Handbook. USA/Canada Christian Ministries Overseas* (Monrovia, Calif.: MARC, 1993).

into two groups: (1) expecting to serve more than 4 years; and (2) expecting to serve 2–11 months. In other words, the meaning of "short-term" was not self-evident. By the same token, it could no longer be taken for granted that long-term meant lifelong service. Not reflected here is the substantial growth in the number of visitors from North America to mission sites around the world, including work parties that spent a few days or weeks assisting with construction or other short-term projects. In the 1980s there was an increasingly strong call for direct congregation-to-congregation relationships, i.e., a congregation in Asia or Africa would enter into direct relationship with a congregation in North America. In this way, it was argued, lay people can participate directly in mission. This change has been greatly facilitated by the ease of international travel and rapid communication. Few were prepared to ask what this shift meant in relation to effective missionary work where the goal was to establish viable congregations. Questions about cultural adaptation, language acquisition, and forming long-lasting relationships across cultural boundaries got pushed aside.

## 1990–1999

In this chapter the development of Mennonite and Brethren in Christ missions has been traced by observing the new missions started in each decade that had church planting as their goal. The story has been dominated by the European and North American agencies, because they have been the agencies charged with responsibility for leading the constituent churches in cross-cultural missions. However, we seem to be on the brink of a decisive shift. In 1999 Mennonite World Conference surveyed the missionary activity of all Anabaptist churches listed in the MWC directory. Not all churches responded and so information remains incomplete.[12] What is reported here is based on actual returns from the churches. Although it is perhaps too early to speak with certainty of a new trend, by comparing information from the 1980s with that of the 1990s we can say that a new stage has been reached.

Compared with each of the decades since 1850, developments in 1990s are nothing less than astonishing. As already noted, the decade of the 1980s had the fewest new missions founded since 1940. Using the information supplied by MWC constituent bodies, we can make the following observations: (1) fifty new missions have been launched over

---

[12] The Beachy Amish/Mennonite Aid, for example, did not reply, but it is known that they have undertaken church planting in several countries.

the past ten years; (2) more than half of these initiatives have been taken by churches in Asia, Africa, and Latin America; and (3) typically these new cross-cultural ventures have been preceded by the development of new churches locally. To move to cross-cultural and international mission initiatives is a significant new stage.

One of the five new missions started in the decade of the 1980s was the witness initiated in Malawi by the Zimbabwean Brethren in Christ Church, in cooperation with the North American BIC Board of Missions. During 1999 the Malawian BIC Church, with a membership of 2,500, has started six new churches in remote areas of the country, and it had under discussion extending its efforts to neighboring Mozambique. At the same time, Brazilian Mennonites are already at work in Mozambique. These are representative of the thirty new initiatives launched by Mennonite and Brethren in Christ churches in Asia, Africa, Europe, and Latin America in the 1990s, involving 500 workers in cross-cultural ministry. In some cases this work is being sponsored in cooperation with a western partner agency, but in other cases the church is raising the needed support from its constituency.

CONCLUSION

Mission has irreversibly changed the Mennonite and Brethren in Christ churches. This revolution has altered these churches in several important ways.

In the first place, the church has discovered a new sense of responsibility for the world. The old search for security was challenged by the call to missionary obedience. The meaning of the gospel has taken on far richer and deeper meaning as we have observed it engaging with multiple contexts throughout the world. It is good news for people the world over.

Second, this opens up new dimensions to our understanding of the nature of the church. Rather than saying that the church has a missionary responsibility, we now know that the church, when true to its nature, is mission. The church without mission is discovered to be a contradiction in terms.

A third feature of this revolution has been the new vision of what the church universal means. The church as a multilingual, multiracial, multicultural peoplehood challenges the old provincialisms. Yet to become such a people requires a miracle, the intervention of divine grace. To actualize this multifaceted church will require that we engage in ministry together. As in a marriage, a relationship only develops as the result of living together.

This leads, in the fourth place, to the challenge to "partnership in the gospel." We can meet in genuine worship and celebration of the church universal only if we are ready to testify to that unity in new missionary obedience and service.

## DEVELOPMENT OF MENNONITE AND BRETHREN IN CHRIST MISSIONS[13]

| | | |
|---|---|---|
| 1851 | Java | DMMA |
| 1871 | Sumatra | DMMA |
| 1890 | Hyderabad, India | MB (Russia) |
| 1898 | S. Rhodesia | BIC |
| | Turkey | MBC |
| 1899 | Madhya Pradesh, India | MBM |
| | Andra Pradesh, India | MB (North America) |
| 1900 | Madhya Pradesh, India | COM |
| 1901 | Shantung, China | KMB (later with EMB, MB, MCA as China Mennonite Mission society) |
| 1905 | Nigeria | MBC |
| 1906 | Zambia | BIC |
| 1908 | W. Bengal, India | MBC |
| 1909 | Hopeh, China | COM |
| 1911 | Fukien, China | MB |
| | Congo | CIM/AIMM |
| 1912 | Congo | MB |
| 1913 | Bihar, India | BIC |
| 1917 | Argentina | MBM |
| 1921 | Inner Mongolia | KMB |
| 1932 | Paraguay | LI (MB Board 1946) |
| 1933 | Mexico | CGCM |
| 1934 | Tanzania | EMM |
| 1935 | Paraguay | MB |
| 1940 | Bihar, India | MBM |
| 1943 | Argentine Chaco | MBM |
| 1945 | Colombia | MB |
| | Colombia | COM |
| | Dominican Republic | MCA |
| | Ecuador | MCA |
| | Sierra Leone | MCA |
| | Puerto Rico | MBM |
| 1946 | Dominican Republic | EMC (US) |

---

[13] Note: The intention has been to include in this list only those new missions started with the goal of developing an organized church. Because of the changing environment, since the 1980s it has become increasingly difficult to obtain consistent information. The old categories no longer serve, but suitable replacements have not been agreed on. The more recent data need further refinement. The information included here suggests trends but should not be treated as being precise. Service projects or instances where personnel have been seconded to another agency—e.g., United Mission to Nepal, collaboration with African Initiated Churches—were not included in the reporting.

| | | |
|---|---|---|
| 1947 | China | MBM |
| 1948 | Ethiopia | EMM |
| 1949 | Irian Jaya | DMMA |
| | Italy | VMBMC/MBM |
| | Jamaica | MCA |
| | Japan | MBM |
| 1950 | Chad | FMMC |
| | Japan | MB |
| | Mexico | COM |
| | Belgium | MBM |
| | Germany | RMM |
| | Honduras | EMM |
| 1951 | Japan | COM |
| 1952 | Haiti | MCA |
| | Alaska | MBM |
| | England | MBM |
| | Cuba | BIC |
| 1953 | Austria | MB |
| | Germany | MB |
| | Japan | BIC |
| | France | MBM |
| | Israel | MBM/EMM |
| | Somalia | EMM |
| | France | EMM |
| 1954 | Cuba | FMC |
| | Taiwan | GC |
| | Mexico | EMC (Can) |
| | Brazil/South | MBM |
| | Uruguay | MBM |
| 1955 | Jamaica | VMBMC |
| | Brazil | MCA |
| | Brazil/North | MBM |
| 1956 | Uruguay | MBM |
| | Ghana | MBM |
| 1957 | Algeria | MBM |
| | Germany | EMM |
| | Vietnam | EMM |
| | Luxembourg | EMM |
| 1958 | Chad | FMMC |
| | Mexico | FMC |
| | Panama | MB |
| 1959 | Paraguay | EMC (Can) |
| | Nigeria | MBM |
| | Mexico | PNMC |
| 1960 | Belize | EMM |
| 1962 | Costa Rica | RMM |
| 1963 | Nigeria | CGCM |
| 1964 | Kenya | EMM |
| 1965 | Nicaragua | BIC |

| | | |
|---|---|---|
| 1965 | Hong Kong | EMM |
| 1966 | Haiti | CGCM |
| | Nicaragua | EMC (Can) |
| 1967 | Ecuador | SMM |
| 1968 | Nicaragua | RMM |
| | Guatemala | EMM/Wash-Frank |
| 1969 | Guyana | VMBMC |
| 1971 | Bolivia | Argentina/MBM/COM |
| | Trinidad-Tobago | VMBMC |
| | Philippines | EMM |
| 1974 | Bangladesh | MB |
| | Philippines | CGCM |
| 1975 | Indonesia | MB/PIPKA |
| | Burkina Faso | CGCM |
| | Germany | EMC (Can) |
| 1976 | Indonesia-Borneo | PIPKA/EMM/MCC |
| | Spain | MB |
| | Spain | MBM/Belgian Mission |
| | Dominican Republic | CGCM |
| | Guatemala | CGCM |
| 1978 | Burkina Faso | AIMM |
| 1980 | Ecuador | RMM |
| 1983 | Malawi | BIC Zimbabwe |
| 1986 | Russia | BTG |
| 1987 | United States | AV |
| 1989 | Singapore | PIPKA |
| 1990 | Burkina Faso | FMMC |
| | Djibouti | MK |
| | Thailand | EMM |
| 1991 | Costa Rica | AV |
| 1992 | Kirghizistan | BTG |
| | Orissa, India | BIC Bihar |
| | Russia | Bielefeld MC |
| 1993 | Albania | EMM |
| | Belarus | BTG |
| | Bolivia | SMM |
| 1994 | Angola | CEM |
| | Laos | FMMC |
| | Lithuania | EMM |
| | Togo | GMC |
| 1995 | Albania | EMC (US) |
| | Canada | MB Paraguay |
| | Mexico | EMC (US) |
| | Middle East | EMC (US) |
| | Nicaragua | AV |
| | Peru | AIMB |
| 1996 | Bolivia | AIMB |
| | Brazil | AV |
| | El Salvador | AV |

| 1996 | Hungary | BTG |
|------|---------|-----|
| | Peru | MB Paraguay |
| | Senegal | AIMM |
| 1997 | Bosnia | AGM |
| | Cambodia | JKI |
| | Ecuador | AMCCR |
| | Germany | EMC (US) |
| | Hong Kong | JKI |
| | India | JKI |
| | Mozambique | BIC Malawi |
| | Nicaragua | MB Paraguay |
| | Venezuela | EMM |
| 1998 | Asian region | SMM |
| | Bolivia | AMCCR |
| | Botswana | BIC Zambia |
| | Canada | JMCC |
| | Ethiopia | DMMK (with MK) |
| | Mexico | AV |
| 1999 | Albania | AEM |
| | Benin | SM |
| | Bolivia | EMB Paraguay |
| | Madagascar | SMM |
| | Mexico | AIMB |
| | Mexico | AMCCR |
| | Mozambique | AEM |
| | Peru | MB Paraguay |
| | Togo | SMM |

## MENNONITE/BRETHREN IN CHRIST MISSIONS FOUNDED 1851–1999 (BY DECADE)

| | |
|-----------|----|
| 1850–1859 | 1 |
| 1870–1879 | 1 |
| 1890–1899 | 5 |
| 1900–1909 | 6 |
| 1910–1919 | 5 |
| 1920–1929 | 1 |
| 1930–1939 | 4 |
| 1940–1949 | 15 |
| 1950–1959 | 38 |
| 1960–1969 | 12 |
| 1970–1979 | 14 |
| 1980–1989 | 5 |
| 1990–1999 | 50 |

SELECTED BIBLIOGRAPHY

Bertsche, James E. *CIM/AIMM: A Story of Vision, Commitment and Grace.* [Elkhart, Ind.?]: Fairway Press, 1998.

*Conrad Grebel Review* 15, no. 1/2 (winter/spring 1997). Issue devoted to the theme "Toward a Global Mennonite/Brethren in Christ Historiography."

Dyck, Cornelius J., ed. *An Introduction to Mennonite History: A Popular History of the Anabaptists and the Mennonites.* Scottdale, Pa.: Herald Press, 1993.

Hege, Nathan. *Beyond Our Prayers: Anabaptist Church Growth in Ethiopia.* Scottdale, Pa.: Herald Press, 1998.

Hess, Mahlon M. *The Pilgrimage of Faith of Tanzania Mennonite Church, 1934–1983.* Salunga, Pa.: Eastern Mennonite Board of Missions and Charities, 1985.

Juhnke, James C. *A People of Mission: A History of General Conference Mennonite Overseas Missions.* Newton, Kans.: Faith and Life Press, 1979.

Lapp, John Allen. *The Mennonite Church In India, 1897–1962.* Scottdale, Pa.: Herald Press, 1972.

Loewen, Melvin J. *Threescore: The Story of an Emerging Mennonite Church in Central Africa.* Elkhart, Ind.: Congo Inland Mission, 1972.

*The Mennonite Encyclopedia.* Numerous articles.

Ramseyer, Robert, and Alice Pannabecker Ramseyer. *Mennonites in China.* Winnipeg: China Educational Exchange, 1988.

Schlabach, Theron F. *Gospel Versus Gospel: Mission and the Mennonite Church.* Scottdale, Pa.: Herald Press, 1980.

Shenk, David W. *Mennonite Safari: The Story of the Mennonite Church in Tanzania.* Scottdale, Pa.: Herald Press, 1974.

Toews, J. B. *The Mennonite Brethren Church in Zaire.* Fresno, Calif.: Board of Christian Literature, Conference of Mennonite Brethren Churches, 1978.

Toews, Jacob J. *The Mennonite Brethren Mission in Latin America.* Board of Christian Literature, General Conference of the Mennonite Brethren Church of North America, 1975.

Yoder, Lawrence M. *The Church of the Muria: A History of the Muria Christian Church of Indonesia—GKMI.* Ann Arbor, Mich.: University Microfilms, 1981.

# 5

## A Global Church Requires a Global History

INTRODUCTION

Around 1970 the world Christian movement crossed an important threshold. That year David B. Barrett predicted that the continent of Africa would have a Christian population of 350 million by the year 2000.[1] Walbert Bühlmann soon followed with his comprehensive survey, *The Coming of the Third Church*.[2] Two centuries after the start of the modern mission movement, the church was more widely dispersed throughout the world than ever before, and the center of gravity of the Christian church was rapidly shifting from the historical heartland in Europe and North America to the southern hemisphere. We still are struggling to understand the ramifications of this development. One dimension that must be addressed is historiography.

When one speaks about the history of the churches in Asia, Africa, and Latin America, in the West it continues to be assumed that this subject falls into the category of mission history. To be sure, the emergence of the church in Asia, Africa, and Latin America in the modern period is intertwined with missions. However, given the fact that scholars and the mass media alike have reduced the missionary and the mission movement to a stereotype, this basic change in identity cannot adequately be comprehended through the category of mission history per se. It is that and much more. The churches of Asia, Africa, and Latin America want to be recognized as full partners with all other churches, not as vassals of foreign patrons as the stereotype implies.

This is a kind of history different from what church historians usually write and teach. This variety traces the founding of the church in

---

Reprinted with permission, with changes, from *Conrad Grebel Review* 15, no. 1/2 (winter/spring 1997): 3–18.

[1] David B. Barrett, "A.D. 2000: 350 Million Christians in Africa," *International Review of Mission* 59 (January 1970): 39–54.

[2] Walbert Bühlmann, *The Coming of the Third Church: An Analysis of the Present and the Future of the Church* (Slough, United Kingdom: St. Paul's Publications, 1976).

those places where it was not present before and its subsequent development in relation to its larger environment. Such history is modeled on the accounts of the church in the New Testament and the post-apostolic period. It pays particular attention to the nature of this initial insertion and the issues raised. Though a church may long since have forgotten the history of its first stage, there can be no church without this founding phase. This history differs from that which studies the settled life of the church in a so-called Christian culture. The latter emphasizes a parochial and institutional view.

To study historical ecclesial reality within its widest and most comprehensive dimensions will entail a double movement. The first move will be to trace the historical development of each local church and its multiple relationships that range from the local to the global. To put it negatively, a historical approach that is limited to the local or national is incomplete. Every local church owes its beginnings to another church, often of a different culture or nationality. The second move entails development of a synthesis that brings the many "locals" into global relationship.

In this essay I propose to review scholarly developments, mainly since 1945, that have contributed to new understandings of ecclesial historiography. Then I will discuss the need for and the possibility of a model for historical work that takes the global church, as it has emerged since the nineteenth century, as the framework for historical investigation and interpretation. We must discard the conventional Christendom framework that holds that normative, and therefore universally determinative Christian history, is what happened as a part of Christendom. Ironically, this assumption has been reinforced by what Theodore H. Von Laue has described as "the world revolution of Westernization" that has seemed to undergird the extension of the western [Christian] tradition worldwide in the modern period.[3] Thirty years ago the Dutch scholar A. T. van Leeuwen offered a theological rationale for this emergence.[4] Today we must interrogate these developments from other angles.

---

[3] Theodore H. Von Laue, *The World Revolution of Westernization: The Twentieth Century in Global Perspective* (New York: Oxford University Press, 1987).

[4] Arend Theodoor van Leeuwen, *Christianity in World History: The Meeting of the Faiths of East and West* (New York: Scribner, 1964).

The history of mission workshop of the 1978 International Association for Mission Studies criticized historians for being "prisoners of their own biases and frames of reference."[5] The criticism was aimed at self-confident western historians of mission who wrote history from the "metropolitan" viewpoint. This distortion, it was argued, can only be overcome by writing church history from multiple perspectives. This and other initiatives will be noted more fully later; but all such efforts have been aimed at redressing imbalances in the histories of particular churches. The object here is to examine the potential of an approach to history that holds the local in its proper relationship with the global.

THE CASE OF THE MENNONITE AND
BRETHREN IN CHRIST CHURCHES, 1850–1995

To establish an empirical base, it is useful to consider what has happened to a particular ecclesiastical tradition as a result of the modern mission movement. Mennonites and Brethren in Christ represent a defined ethnic group that has been substantially changed by mission. Although this case is not unique, it serves to ground the discussion in experience.

Four sets of data outline in broad strokes the state of Mennonite/Brethren in Christ reality as of 1850, the process of expansion over the next 145 years, and the present status measured in terms of membership.

*Membership in 1850*

In 1850 constituent churches were found in eight nations: Austria, Canada, France, Germany, the Netherlands, Russia, Switzerland, and the United States. Total membership was approximately 120,000 baptized adults of European extraction.

*Membership in 1911*

| Europe and Russia | 150,000 |
|---|---|
| North America | 76,746 |
| Asia, Africa | 3,000 |
| Total (est.) baptized membership | 229,746 |

---

[5] Godwin O. M. Tasie, Joan Chatfield, Bong Rin Ro, and Oscar Beozzo, "History of Mission: Urgent Research Fields; Role of Women in Mission," *Missiology* 7 (January 1979): 92–96.

## Growth of Overseas Missions

Dutch Mennonites took the first step in overseas missions in 1851 when they sent a missionary couple to Indonesia. Mennonite missions overseas grew slowly until 1945; thereafter, a surge of new initiatives resulted in the founding of churches on all continents.

| Period | Number of missions founded |
|---|---|
| 1850–1869 | 1 |
| 1870–1889 | 1 |
| 1890–1899 | 5 |
| 1900–1909 | 7 |
| 1910–1919 | 4 |
| 1920–1929 | 1 |
| 1930–1944 | 6 |
| 1945–1959 | 52 |
| 1960–1969 | 11 |
| 1970–1992 | 38 |

## World Membership

| | 1978 | 1984 | 1990 | 1994 |
|---|---|---|---|---|
| Africa | 85,900 | 107,300 | 176,500 | 276,653 |
| Asia | 74,300 | 113,600 | 147,600 | 151,057 |
| Latin America | 44,300 | 75,300 | 83,400 | 91,436* |
| Europe | 96,100 | 92,700 | 68,600 | 49,132 |
| North America | 313,000 | 340,000 | 380,500 | 405,713 |
| Total | 613,600 | 728,900 | 856,600 | 973,991 |

Given the more rapid rate of growth outside the West, membership in Asia, Africa, and Latin America where mission efforts had been concentrated since 1851 surpassed that of the historical heartland in Europe and North America by the end of the twentieth century. By any reckoning, this represents a massive redefinition in Mennonite identity. In view of this growth, and consequent expanded identity, what changes on the part of sociologists and historians are called for if they are to understand and interpret this new situation comprehensively? Fortunately, we have a variety of resources with which to work at reconceptualizing the historical task.

---

* Includes members of mission-founded congregations (48,768) and of European Mennonite immigrant congregations (42,668). The latter group consists of 13,456 members of churches affiliated with Mennonite World Conference, plus 29,212 Old Colony Mennonites.

EMERGENT PERSPECTIVES

Some of the groundwork for a revised approach to interpreting ecclesial reality is already in place. Certain historians have demonstrated both the justification for and the potential of fresh approaches to the modern mission movement as an important episode in human experience. In some cases historians, with no confessional intent, have helped to break down the largely self-imposed parochialism that has characterized ecclesiastical historiography. A parallel development has been the reevaluation of the processes by which the Christian faith is transmitted and which lead to the establishment of the church on new soil.

*Historical Studies*

There has been no lack of historical writing critical of the role of the West in relation to the rest of the world. To the extent that Christian missions have been included in these accounts, they have been treated as willing accomplices of western expansion to other continents. Both western and nonwestern scholars have produced such works. An exemplar of this disposition is the Indian historian-diplomat K. M. Panikkar. In his critical survey of the role of Europe in Asia during the 450-year "Vasco da Gama epoch," Panikkar devoted a brief chapter to the work of Christian missions and their results. Portraying Christian missionaries as little more than pawns in the hands of the colonial powers, he concluded: "It cannot be denied that the attempt to convert Asia has definitely failed."[6] Writing soon after the closing of China in 1949, Panikkar required no great imagination to see missionary work in Asia as a singular failure. He suggested that this failure of missions had been even more complete than necessary and adduced five reasons for this rout: (1) the attitude of moral superiority which stained all that the missionary touched, (2) the indubitable link between missionary work and the imperialist project, (3) the attitude of cultural superiority that marked all aspects of the western incursion into other cultures, (4) the disunity among Christians, and (5) the rise of unbelief in Europe and the crisis in European culture represented by World War 1 and the Bolshevik revolution that undermined the credibility of things Christian. It has long been taken for granted that Christian missions have about them the bad odor of failure. Such critical works are essential to our understanding of

---

[6] K. M. Panikkar, *Asia and Western Dominance: A Survey of the Vasco da Gama Epoch of Asian History, 1498–1945* (London: George Allen and Unwin, 1959; first edition, 1953), 297.

how the church has been viewed and Christian initiatives evaluated. These criticisms have substance.

Yet fresh scholarly work by both ecclesiastical and secular scholars has been eroding this consensus. Reconsideration has been encouraged by such figures as John King Fairbank, long-time sinologist at Harvard. In his presidential address to the American Historical Association in 1968, Fairbank argued that "the missionary in foreign parts seems to be the invisible man of American history.... Missionaries went out from most of Europe and the British Commonwealth as well as from the United States; ...they worked in the most diverse lands abroad, encountering widely different societies and institutions. Mission history is a great and underused research laboratory for the comparative observation of cultural stimulus and response in both directions."[7] Fairbank was no apologist for Christian missions, but he saw the huge untapped resource for studying intercultural relations that was locked away in mission archives. Especially noteworthy is his emphasis on the reciprocal action inherent in intercultural relations. Fairbank was sensitive to subtleties of human relations that cannot be accounted for by the old interpretive framework. He encouraged historians to set aside their prejudices so that they might exploit the extensive untapped raw materials generated by modern missions. The odds were they would discover a far more complex and interesting account of relationships between the West and other parts of the world than the old stereotypes had allowed.

On another front, Andrew Porter has been researching a particularly sensitive phase in Christian history, the high imperial period and its aftermath.[8] Porter has probed the influences that contributed to the formation of missionaries in their home environment, the combination of socioeconomic and political forces that spawned and drove imperialism, and the caliber and role of missionary statecraft. Porter's studies reveal a

---

[7] John K. Fairbank, "Assignment for the '70's," *American Historical Review* 74 (February 1969): 877–78.

[8] Andrew Porter, "Cambridge, Keswick, and Late Nineteenth-Century Attitudes to Africa," *Journal of Imperial and Commonwealth History* 5 (1976): 5–34; Andrew Porter, "Evangelical Enthusiasm, Missionary Motivation, and West Africa in the Late Nineteenth Century: The Career of G. W. Brooke," *Journal of Imperial and Commonwealth History* 6 (1977): 23–46; Andrew Porter, "Religion and Empire: British Expansion in the Long Nineteenth Century, 1780–1914," *Journal of Imperial and Commonwealth History* 20 (1992): 370–90.

more nuanced and multivalent phenomenon than has been depicted in the
past.

## Mission Studies

A young French Reformed missionary named Maurice Leenhardt went to
New Caledonia as a missionary in 1902, determined to strive for
religious authenticity in his work as evangelist and Bible translator.[9]
Resisting pressure from his supporters at home, including his own
mother, Leenhardt refused to sentimentalize, and thereby distort, the
responses of the New Caledonians to the Christian message. Yet he also
declined to accept conventional ethnography as the grid through which to
interpret Melanesian life. He came to appreciate the complex and
multilayered nature of conversion in Melanesian culture. This
appreciation required rigorous examination of both sending and receptor
cultures and of the interface between the two. As a Bible translator he
grappled with how to express "God" in the categories of New
Caledonian thought. Leenhardt recognized that he could not be effective
as an evangelist and translator unless he was prepared to participate in
"acculturation in two directions"; that is, he must be willing to be
co-participant with the New Caledonians in the evangelization process.
He represents a genre of missionaries that helped relativize the position
of the western missionary vis-à-vis the host people.

Another step was a basic change in the evaluation of indigenous
Christian movements. This opened the way to the introduction of
non-Christendom categories and standards. Some of the most influential
works contributing to this reorientation have been based on experiences
in Africa. A pioneering study is Bengt Sundkler's *Bantu Prophets in
South Africa*.[10] Prior to Sundkler's work, the conventional wisdom held
that indigenous versions of Christianity in Africa—described variously
as Zionist, prophetic, separatist, or independent churches—were aberrant
forms that must be rejected. Sundkler studied these movements on their
own terms and concluded they may be regarded as authentic expressions
of Christian faith.

---

[9] James Clifford, "The Translation of Cultures," *Journal of Pacific History* 15
(1980): 3, 6, 7; and James Clifford, *Person and Myth: Maurice Leenhardt in the
Melanesian World* (Berkeley, Calif.: University of California Press, 1982), 65–
68, 77–82.

[10] Bengt Sundkler, *Bantu Prophets in South Africa* (London: Oxford University
Press, 1961; first edition, 1948).

From another angle, Roland Oliver's *The Missionary Factor in East Africa*[11] modeled a rethinking of the role of the missionary in East Africa by placing the movement in its wider social and political context, with African actors taking important roles in the drama. Oliver set a new standard and demonstrated the value of an approach that moved away from institutional or promotional histories characteristic of mission historiography up to that time.

Oliver's study was soon augmented by the seminal work of missionary scholar John V. Taylor, *The Growth of the Church in Buganda*. Taylor traced the emergence of the church among a particular people and attempted to take both the missionary and the Baganda seriously, allowing for greater parity between Christendom and emerging African theology. Taylor was deeply impressed by the differences in perception, honestly and sincerely held by both missionary and Baganda, that influenced communication. According to Taylor:

> It appears that there is an incalculable gap between the Gospel that is proclaimed and the Gospel that is heard, which has not always been taken into account in discussions about evangelism.... From the time of C. T. Wilson to the present day, the Christian message has been preached with all the special emphases of Moravian and Anglican Evangelical theology—the sinful condition of man, the Atonement and the Saviourhood of Christ, the conversion of the individual through conscious repentance and faith, and the offer of sanctification through the Holy Spirit conditioned by the surrender of the believer's will. Yet the message which was received and implanted and upon which the church in Buganda was founded, was primarily news about the transcendent God. 'Katonda', the unknown and scarcely heeded Creator, was proclaimed as the focus of all life, who yet lay beyond and above the closed unity of all existence.... It was as though the missionaries preached Paul's gospel to Corinth, but their converts heard Paul's sermon to the Athenians mingled with Isaiah's message to the city of Jerusalem.[12]

Notwithstanding this "miscommunication," a life-altering process was set in motion, and thousands of Baganda people would respond to this message over the next decades. Who would dare to say they did not

---

[11] Roland Anthony Oliver, *The Missionary Factor in East Africa* (London: Longmans, Green and Co., 1965; first edition, 1952).

[12] Taylor, John V. *The Growth of the Church in Buganda: An Attempt at Understanding* (London: SCM Press, 1958), 252–53.

hear "gospel," even if what they apprehended was quite different from what the missionaries thought they were preaching? Communication, with far-reaching consequences, did take place. Was the message the Baganda heard any less valid than what the missionaries intended that they receive? The Baganda contextualized the gospel in their culture as only cultural insiders can do, and the result was that they now acclaimed Jesus Christ as Lord. Is the Christian *ecumené* impoverished or enriched by such diversity in hearing the gospel?

With his study of religious independency in East Africa, F. B. Welbourn contributed further to this shift in the focus of historical investigation from a strictly Euro-centric, unidirectional approach, to one of reciprocity and interaction. "The purpose of this discussion," wrote Welbourn, "is to insist that African response to missionary endeavour cannot be seen simply as a 'religious' response to a purely religious message."[13] African cultures do not divide sacred from profane. The African intuitively responded out of a whole culture worldview and expected the European to do the same. The African could not understand the Christian faith in isolation from the European culture in which it came garbed. The fragmented nature of modern western culture, which defined the worldview of missionaries from the West, was itself at issue in all attempts at intercultural relations. The cross-cultural communication of the Christian message proved to be more complex than had been understood earlier.

Studies by European scholars continued to multiply, but an important new phase was emerging. In the 1960s Africans began earning doctorates under Roland Oliver, Andrew Walls, Richard Gray, and others, and soon were publishing their own books and essays. Authoritative new studies of Christian history in Africa by Africans began appearing: works by Ajayi,[14] Ayandele,[15] Ekechi,[16] and Tasie,[17] to

---

[13] Frederick Burkewood Welbourn, *East African Rebels: A Study of Some Independent Churches* (London: SCM Press, 1961), 177.

[14] J. F. Ade Ajayi, *Christian Missions in Nigeria, 1841–1891: The Making of a New Élite* (Evanston: Northwestern University Press, 1965).

[15] Emmanuel Ayankanmi Ayandele, *The Missionary Impact on Modern Nigeria, 1842–1914: A Political and Social Analysis* (London: Longmans, Green and Co., 1966).

[16] Felix K. Ekechi, *Missionary Enterprise and Rivalry in Igboland, 1857–1914* (London: Frank Cass, 1972).

name a few. This has resulted in a fresh reading of history, based on primary sources housed in the archives of missionary societies and church bodies, in Europe and in Africa, which challenged the insular and one-sided view that characterized histories written by western scholars for a largely western audience.

In their provocative essay, "Writing African Church History," Ajayi and Ayandele argued: "A bitter pill which the majority of writers on Christianity and missionary activities should swallow is that they have not been writing African Church History."[18] Ajayi and Ayandele insisted on a radical definition: "An African Church must necessarily be the product of an organic growth on the African soil, an institution in which Christianity is incarnate within the African milieu."[19] They took umbrage at the assumption held by the majority of scholars that mission-established churches could be authentically African—indeed, were taken to be the norm by which the "Christianness" of indigenous forms was to be judged. Ajayi and Ayandele contended that mission-founded churches "remain essentially imitations of their mothers in Europe and America."[20] Against this one-sided view, they cited the observation by Bishop James Johnson, a Sierra Leonean who served the church in Nigeria, who said in 1905, "Christianity is a religion intended for and is suitable for every Race and Tribe of people on the face of the Globe."[21] Johnson was appealing for equality and mutual respect between Africans and Europeans; but he was swimming against the rising tide of European imperialism and racism, as well as against the entrenched assumption that privileged historical Christendom is the fountain of spiritual truth, authority, and normativity.

Inevitably, this resulted in historical distortion inasmuch as it screened out of consideration the indispensable role of indigenous

---

[17] G. O. M. Tasie, *Christian Missionary Enterprise in the Niger Delta, 1864–1918* (Leiden: E. J. Brill, 1978).

[18] Ajayi and Ayandele, "Writing African Church History," in *The Church Crossing Frontiers: Essays on the Nature of the Church,* ed. Peter Beyerhaus and Carl F. Hallencreutz (Uppsala: Gleerup, 1966). Cf. M. R. Spindler, "Writing African Church History (1969–1989): A Survey of Recent Studies," *Exchange* 19 (April 1990): 1–15.

[19] Ajayi and Ayandele, "Writing African Church History," 90.

[20] Ibid., 91.

[21] Ibid.

Christians in the evangelization of their own peoples from the earliest stages of Christian witness. The roles of catechists, evangelists, and Bible women, as well as lay people who used their professions as vehicles for Christian witness, remain largely unexplored, in part because of inadequate documentation but more importantly because they have been ignored. Yet without them the story of Christian expansion since 1800 would have been different, if, indeed, there would be much of a story at all.[22]

Ajayi and Ayandele recognized the important work of European scholars in breaking down longstanding prejudices. They note the work of Sundkler (mentioned above), and Harold W. Turner's thorough study of a single indigenous church, the Church of the Lord (Aladura).[23] But the main thrust of their essay was to describe a program for the reinterpretation of Christianity in Africa by Africans.

African historical and religious studies flourished in the 1960s and 1970s. Innovative research and writing was promoted by scholars such as T. O. Ranger, J. F. A. Ajayi, and E. Mveng, who understood the need to devise approaches geared to the particularities of Africa's historical and cultural realities.[24] The integral role of religion in African cultural history was stressed.[25]

This survey might leave the impression that we should be satisfied that African churches have gained the freedom to work out their own salvation unfettered by western conventions and prejudices. But, as Andrew Walls has reminded us, the dynamic growth of the church in Africa in the twentieth century is forging a new theological agenda for which there are no ready answers. Indeed, African theologians may well discover and "develop aspects of the Biblical material which Western theology has left undeveloped simply because Western society was

---

[22] Cf. Lamin O. Sanneh, *West African Christianity: The Religious Impact* (Maryknoll: Orbis Books, 1983), chap. 7.

[23] Harold W. Turner, *History of an African Independent Church*, 2 vols. (Oxford: Clarendon Press, 1967).

[24] See T. O. Ranger, "Resolutions," in *Emerging Themes in African History*, ed. T. O. Ranger (Nairobi: East Africa Publishing House, 1968), 218–22.

[25] Cf. T. O. Ranger and Isaria N. Kimambo, eds., *The Historical Study of African Religion* (Berkeley: University of California Press, 1972).

culturally unable to see them."[26] In working out its theological response to African realities, the church in Africa will thereby expand and enrich the understanding of the whole church.

We could as readily have drawn observations from the experiences of the churches in Latin America and Asia. All point to the same conclusion: an archaic and monolithic Christendom could not be adapted to the cultures of Asia, Africa, and Latin America. The Christian faith itself requires that the mystery of the Incarnation be recapitulated in each cultural environment. Only in this way, and notwithstanding the incalculable risks that vernacularization of the gospel entails, could the genius of the faith be preserved. If this is granted, then the investigation and interpretation of this historical process cannot be executed faithfully when that process is confined to the assumptions and approaches of historical Christendom. The changed reality we have been describing means that the very form and ethos of the church have been substantially transformed as the result of its dispersion "to the uttermost parts of the world."

INITIATIVES TOWARD NEW CHURCH HISTORIES

The vision of Ajayi and Ayandele was shared by a growing number of people. Scholars in Asia, Africa, and Latin America increasingly insisted that each church deserved to have its history written by a historian whose roots were in that church. Two notable projects were organized in 1973 for the purpose of preparing multivolume histories of the churches in the Indian subcontinent and in Latin America. Both projects were designed to cover the entire history of Christianity in that region and therefore were to be ecumenical in scope and in execution.

*Church History Association of India*

In October 1973 the Church History Association of India formed an editorial board and designed a six-volume history of Christianity in India to be written by a team of scholars drawn from the Protestant, Roman Catholic, and Mar Thoma communities. The official statement said, "The history of Christianity in India has hitherto often been treated as an eastward extension of western ecclesiastical history."[27] This treatment

---

[26] A. F. Walls, "Towards Understanding Africa's Place in Christian History," in *Religion in a Pluralistic Society: Essays Presented to Professor C. G. Baëta,* ed. J. S. Pobee (Leiden: E. J. Brill, 1976), 184.

[27] "A Scheme for a Comprehensive History of Christianity in India," in *Indian Church History* 8 (1974): 89–90. John C. B. Webster, "The History of

led to one of two extremes: the history of the church has been seen either from an entirely internal and parochial viewpoint, or as a foreign mission. Both results have reinforced the notion that Christianity is alien to Indian soil. What is needed is history that locates the church firmly in the Indian historical context. The project set for itself a double task: to reevaluate existing materials and to conduct fresh research. The perspective adopted consisted of four dimensions: (1) the sociocultural (to demonstrate the integral relationship between Christianity and the wider Indian society), (2) the regional (out of consideration of substantial regional or local social and cultural diversities within India), (3) the national as the main framework for interpretation, and (4) the ecumenical, i.e., Christianity *in toto* rather than one particular form of it. (Denominational distinctives were not to be ignored but were not to be treated as primary.) To date, four volumes have been published.

*Latin American Project*

In 1973 the Roman Catholic Bishops' Council of Latin America authorized the founding of the Comision de Estudios de Historia de la Iglesia en America Latina (CEHILA). This was conceived as an "ecumenical effort on a regional level" that would "research church history from the perspective of the people evangelized as well as from that of the bishops, clergy and missionaries involved."[28] Whereas in the past the primary concern had been to obtain adequate and reliable documentation, now the issue was held to be "the pervasive presence of bias inherent in all historical data.... All chroniclers spin their own thread and weave their own categories. None are objective."[29] The CEHILA plan called for an eleven-volume history of Christianity in Latin America written in Spanish by an ecumenical team headed by Enrique Dussel.

The five centuries of history of the church in Latin America have been marked by great inner tensions because the church has been involved both in the process of conquest and in protest and resistance against it. In his introduction to *The Church in Latin America, 1492–*

---

Christianity in India: Aims and Methods," *Bangalore Theological Forum* 10 (1978): 110–48, gives a masterly overview of ecclesiastical historiography in India over the past 150 years.

[28] Tasie, "History of Mission," 93.

[29] Ibid.

*1992,* prepared for the 500th anniversary of Columbus's arrival in the Americas, Dussel wrote:

> The programme of the historical mission of the founder of Christianity is at the same time the mission or essence of the church. This programme was set out by Jesus when he unrolled the scroll containing the book of Isaiah [Luke 4:16–21].... If 'bringing good news to the poor' was his specific historical purpose and that of his church, this must also be the absolute and primary criterion of a *Christian* interpretation of the history of that church—a scientific interpretation, certainly, but also Christian (based on faith).[30]

The work of CEHILA is noteworthy for its analytical rigor and comprehensiveness. It reflects the critical dynamic unleashed within the Latin American churches since 1968 and since the emergence of liberation theology.

ECUMENICAL INITIATIVES IN HISTORIOGRAPHY[31]

Two broadly ecumenical initiatives emerged in the late 1970s, bringing together theologians from the main ecclesiastical traditions. The first was the Ecumenical Association of Third World Theologians (EATWOT), which over the past eighteen years has convened a series of conferences around themes of concern to the churches of Africa, Asia, and Latin America. A second initiative was a conference held in Basel in 1981 on "Church History in an Ecumenical Perspective," sponsored by Swiss church historians.[32] In 1983 EATWOT created its Working Commission on Church History in the Third World, with Enrique Dussel of Mexico as coordinator. By 1989 this commission had sponsored five consultations.[33] Proceedings of two meetings have been published.[34]

---

[30] Enrique Dussel, ed., *The Church in Latin America, 1492–1992* (Maryknoll: Orbis Books, 1992), 1.

[31] These initiatives arise largely out of the Protestant-led ecumenical movement. Roman Catholic historiography traditionally had a distinctive understanding of the history of the church and Christianity. See Hubert Jedin's general introduction to church history in *From the Apostolic Community to Constantine,* by Karl Baus, vol. 1, *Handbook of Church History,* ed. Hubert Jedin (New York: Herder and Herder, 1965).

[32] Lukas Vischer, ed., *Church History in an Ecumenical Perspective* (Bern: Evangelische Arbeitsstelle Oekumene Schweiz, 1982).

[33] Consultations were held in 1983, 1984, 1985, 1986, 1987, and 1989. The 1989 consultation laid plans for three symposia treating the history of the church in Asia, Africa, and Latin America, with each volume edited by a scholar from that

Instead of the ecumenical perspective of the 1981 meeting, attention shifted to Third World church history. This is an important task, and much work remains to be done with regard to it.[35] Yet the task will not be completed when Third World church history has been written; a further challenge remains.

## THE CHALLENGE OF WRITING GLOBAL CHURCH HISTORY

Each of the developments we have surveyed has been an important advance. What is now needed is to conceptualize and produce a global history.

A history of the Christian movement based on a global perspective must surmount several hurdles.

### The Burden of the Past

In spite of the ferment and innovations in the study of Christian history over the past several decades, the undertow of tradition remains strong. In the West, for example, church histories continue to be written and church history is taught with little serious attention to the majority church, i.e., the church outside historical Christendom.[36] This attitudinal and conceptual barrier is linked to another one, the ingrained bias against mission. Despite the fact that the mission dynamic since 1800 has brought about this sea change in Christian identity, many Christian scholars treat mission with diffidence. This makes the task of historical interpretation even more critical, for the future of the church is

---

continent. To date the volume on Latin America (Dussel, *The Church in Latin America*) is the only one to be published. Thanks to Gerald H. Anderson for supplying this information.

[34] Lukas Vischer, ed., *Towards a History of the Church in the Third World: Papers and Report of a Consultation on the Issue of Periodisation Convened by the Working Commission on Church History of the Ecumenical Association of Third World Theologians* (Bern: Evangelische Arbeitsstelle Oekumene Schweiz, 1985). Ogbu K. Kalu, ed., *African Church Historiography: An Ecumenical Perspective* (Bern: Evangelische Arbeitsstelle Oekumene Schweiz, 1988).

[35] Cf. Carl F. Hallencreutz, "Third World Church History—An Integral Part of Theological Education," *Studia Theologica* 47 (1993): 29–47; and John Schumacher, "The 'Third World' and the Self-Understanding of the Twentieth-Century Church," in *History: Self-Understanding of the Church,* ed. Roger Aubert (New York: Herder and Herder, 1971), 102–11.

[36] Cf. Andrew F. Walls, "Structural Problems in Mission Studies," *International Bulletin of Missionary Research* 15, no. 4 (October 1991): 146–55.

inseparable from the mission dynamic. Where mission consciousness is extinguished, the church languishes and atrophies.

## A Model for Intercultural History

Another way of speaking about global history is to describe it as intercultural history. To succeed, intercultural history must ensure that each member group is fairly represented so that the integrity of the whole is maintained. To work out this perspective will entail confronting deeply held habits of heart and mind. But we are impelled toward this ideal precisely out of a desire to tell the history of the Christian movement as truthfully as possible. Every account that parochializes the history of the church suppresses the full truth. We need models and methodologies that will help us to elucidate the truth of the whole. At several points we have noted suggestive examples.

One cluster of insights arrived at by thoughtful missionaries, social scientists, and historians has concerned intercultural communication and relationship. Leenhardt used the term "acculturation in two directions"; Fairbank spoke of "cultural stimulus and response in both directions." Another concept that has been employed effectively is that of translation.[37] The translation model is highly suggestive. No one can translate into a language that is not one's mother tongue independent of native speakers. Even the most gifted linguist remains dependent on mother-tongue informants. This becomes especially true when one enters the realm of religious faith, as was illustrated by John V. Taylor's investigation into the church in Buganda. The only recourse is to admit one's dependence on others. Though a translator may not be fully aware of such dependence, translation cannot proceed without continual assistance. Each time the translator asks, "What does this mean," a concession has been made to the authority of the native speaker and power has been ceded to the other. The only way forward is to accept a relationship of reciprocity and mutual dependence. This model sets the stage for sound relationship by focusing on interdependence and mutual benefit, rather than on preserving the power prerogative of one party over the other. Ultimately, the host people will decide how much of the

---

[37] Clifford, *Person and Myth*; Lamin Sanneh, *Translating the Message: The Missionary Impact on Culture* (Maryknoll: Orbis Books, 1989); and Lamin Sanneh, "Mission and the Modem Imperative—Retrospect and Prospect: Charting a Course," in *Earthen Vessels: American Evangelicals and Foreign Missions, 1880–1980,* ed. Joel A. Carpenter and Wilbert R Shenk (Grand Rapids: Wm. B. Eerdmans Publishing Co., 1990), 301–16.

message they will accept and in what forms.[38] That is, they must take
responsibility for its contextualization in their lives, as did the Baganda.
This model may provide us with a starting point for investigating
intercultural relationships over time that can overcome the sterile
stereotypes governing historical research and writing in past decades.

*Developing a Global Approach*

Paul A. Cohen concludes his provocative and illuminating investigation
of how the history of China has been written over the past 150 years by
recommending that a China-centered approach be adopted in the future.[39]
Cohen's suggestions can be adapted to our quest for a global church
history. His approach has four characteristics:

1.   Chinese history begins in China rather than in the West. Cohen
insists, as far as possible, on internal (Chinese) rather than external
(western) criteria as the basis "for determining what is historically
significant in the Chinese past." Applying this to a global church history
means we must resolutely reject western Christendom as the starting
point.

2.   It regards China "horizontally" in terms of discrete units—
regions, provinces, prefectures, cities—to demonstrate that power flows
in multiple directions. Applying this to a global church history allows us
to show the parity between the local and global. The history of the
church is a search for understanding of the life and growth of the church
in time and space throughout the world; each local, regional, or national
unit of the church is incomplete in and of itself.

3.   It separates Chinese society "vertically" into discrete levels and
encourages the writing of history that is accessible to the wider populace.
Applying this to a global history will involve using various media for
making the history of the church available so that it serves the whole
people, not only the specialists.

4.   It embraces theories, methodologies, and techniques developed
in other disciplines, especially the social sciences, that can be integrated
into historical analysis. Applying this to a global church history means

---

[38] An eloquent example of this approach is recounted by Vincent J. Donovan,
*Christianity Rediscovered: An Epistle from the Masai* (Maryknoll: Orbis Books,
1978).

[39] Paul A. Cohen, *Discovering History in China: American Historical Writing
on the Recent Chinese Past* (New York: Columbia University Press, 1984).

that social history and narrative will be essential building blocks in constructing the historical account.

## Marks of a Global Church History

What criteria may we use to determine whether we are moving toward our ideal of a history that is truly global in spirit and in substance? Four marks present themselves:

1.  Global church history will enable adherents from diverse backgrounds to embrace the larger story as "our history" because it clarifies their identity as members of a common—though culturally variegated—narrative over time.

2.  Global church history will demonstrate that the local is essential to the global; there is no global apart from the local.

3.  Global church history will recognize the power of social history and narrative to create a universally meaningful story. The global dimension remains abstract and distant until it is grounded in a narrative.

4.  Global church history will illuminate the meaning of the church precisely in its capacity to incarnate the life of God as revealed in Jesus Christ among all peoples in all places and in all times. It fosters cultural authenticity combined with ecclesial unity.

## "NEW OCCASIONS DEMAND NEW DUTIES"

This, then, is the challenge that a global approach to church history puts to us: the church at the end of the twentieth century faces an extraordinary opportunity that is the fruit of an extraordinary epoch of growth and change. Over the past two hundred years the identity of the Christian church has been redefined. The center of gravity is now in the south rather than the north. This historical shift and its manifold implications have immense importance for the future of the church. The urgent priority we face today is to understand and interpret this development.

# 6

## A Traditioned Theology of Mission

INTRODUCTION

Nearly all theology of mission produced in the past fifty years may be characterized as generic. That is to say, theology of mission has not been related to a particular theological tradition. This may be regarded as a positive development inasmuch as theologians of mission have devoted their efforts to laying a foundation for missionary obedience by the whole church. But this is an anomaly when placed in the context of theology generally. Numerous theologies treating a range of pastoral topics, evangelism, ethics, and systematic theology have been produced by and for particular theological traditions. Why is it not appropriate to work out a theology of mission on foundational themes of a theological tradition?

In fact, we may put the challenge more forcefully: The validity of any theology can be established only by its proven effectiveness in assisting the church in fulfilling its missionary obligation in the world. And this requirement can only be met when a particular church puts its theological convictions to the test in missionary practice. A theology of mission is essential if the church is to formulate its theological position with this missionary purpose as its aim.

With this goal in mind, I propose to survey and summarize the themes that have emerged from the theological reflection on missionary engagement by Mennonites in the period since 1970. This is the traditioned theology of mission I am presenting.

To set this work in its proper context, we must first clarify the definitions of "Anabaptist" and "Mennonite." These terms are often used imprecisely and loosely. I contend that the reality with which we have to deal today is Mennonite rather than Anabaptist, and that we should not confuse the two, especially when we are discussing theology of mission.

---

Part of this chapter is reprinted with permission, with changes, from Calvin E. Shenk, ed., *A Relevant Anabaptist Missiology for the 1990s* (Elkhart, Ind.: Council of International Ministries, 1990).

In the second section I examine the various sources of a Mennonite theology of mission. This will show that this emerging theology of mission is heavily dependent on modern sources. Nonetheless, these recent efforts have intentionally combined insights from biblical studies, Anabaptist studies, Mennonite history, and the contemporary theology of mission in articulating a theology of mission to serve the Mennonite tradition. These theological labors have come after more than a century of missionary work, both at home and abroad, and more than fifty years after the launching of the movement to "recover" the Anabaptist vision.

We begin, therefore, with a clarification of the terms that figure importantly in our study: "Anabaptist" and "Mennonite." Historical Anabaptism is not synonymous with contemporary Mennonitism. Anabaptism can be defined in terms of at least six dimensions.

### "Anabaptism"

*1.* Anabaptism is a *historical* phenomenon. Anabaptism is a specific religious reform movement of the sixteenth century. It represents one stream that flowed within the wider Reformation. Anabaptism is that part of the Reformation variously called the Radical or Left Wing because of its thoroughgoing criticism of established views, values, and institutions, both Roman Catholic and Protestant.

*2.* Anabaptism is a *theological* stance. In common with other Christian traditions, Anabaptists affirmed the foundational doctrines of the Christian faith. In addition, they called for a more rigorous application of the teachings of Jesus by their emphasis on discipleship as *Nachfolge*, the church as a voluntary community (rather than being linked to the state), and the way of love in human relations.

*3.* We may define Anabaptism *ecclesiastically*. Anabaptists had broken away from Roman Catholicism but were also out of step with the main Reformers. The Anabaptists stressed that the goal of reform was to restore the New Testament church. They saw themselves as representing a "third way" that was neither Protestant nor Roman Catholic.

*4.* *Ethics* was of crucial importance. The Anabaptist conception of ethics placed the movement at odds with other Christian traditions. They believed the life and teachings of Jesus to be normative for Christian discipleship. Followers of Jesus were to renounce the use of violence. Certain vocations were incompatible with Christian discipleship. Ethics informed vocation.

*5.* Anabaptism was marked by a strong *missionary consciousness*. For the Anabaptists it was crucial that the church maintain a missionary stance vis-à-vis the world, the realm where spiritual and human reality did not consciously submit to the reign of Jesus Christ. Indeed, this was considered to be the normal self-understanding of the church. The faithful church expected to live in tension with the world, and the absence of such tension was a sign of apostasy.

     *6.* "Anabaptist" and "Anabaptism" also have a *contemporary* usage. In recent years the term has increasingly entered into the vocabulary of those groups that trace some lineal descent from the sixteenth-century Anabaptists and that wish to identify themselves as a part of this stream. Sometimes it is used to encompass the wider Mennonite/Brethren in Christ constituency. At other times it is a designation for certain contemporary renewal movements that consider themselves neo-Anabaptist. On other occasions it is a convenient trans-denominational label applied without regard to theological identity. When a term is used in such an elastic and imprecise fashion it is no longer functional.

*"Mennonitism"*

We now turn to a contrasting set of definitions of "Mennonite" or "Mennonitism." For purposes of comparison we will use the categories we applied to Anabaptism.

     *1.* Speaking *historically* and *sociologically,* Mennonitism, as it evolved in the seventeenth century, was what survived the persecution of the Anabaptists in the sixteenth century. The price of survival was to come to terms with the larger society, that is, the world. In other words, survival was contingent on accommodation to the demands and reality of society at large. Except in the Netherlands, Mennonitism adopted as its primary strategy withdrawal from society in exchange for the possibility of pursuing its own agenda.

     Internally, Mennonitism fortified itself for survival through ethnic cohesiveness and a system of group controls characteristic of any socioethnic group. Societies of this sort generally guard against innovation and change. The outsider who enters such a society will be required to undergo cultural circumcision and conform to the group.

     Innovation was threatening, yet it did come as the result of interaction with the larger society and with other churches. Typically, some trusted individual who was able to stand on the margin of Mennonitism and interact with outside groups became the channel for mediating innovation within the Mennonite community. This led to various changes—economic, geographical (i.e., migration), theological, and spiritual. Significantly, the Anabaptist legacy did not serve as the basis for renewal and change. Instead the early confessions of faith and *The Martyrs Mirror* were used to warn against innovations out of fear of compromise. Not until the twentieth century, as a result of the "recovery" movement, did it come to be expected that the heirs of the Anabaptists might find in sixteenth-century experience resources for the renewal of the church.

*2.* The *theological* identity of Mennonitism is essentially that of conservative Protestant orthodoxy, albeit noncreedal in formulation, with a bias toward biblicism and a mistrust of systematic and formal theologies. Particularly from the nineteenth century on, as Mennonites began to mingle more widely with other Christians and accommodated to the dominant culture, they have taken their cues in theology and piety largely from the evangelical mainstream.

*3.* In terms of *ecclesiastical* relations, Mennonites, in contrast to Anabaptists, identify strongly with Protestantism in its severe critique of Roman Catholic sacerdotalism and sacramentalism, yet share with Catholicism its strong sense of the church and its discipline. A major source of Mennonite distinctiveness has been ethnic cohesion and cultural identity, as well as lay ministry, nonliturgical worship, and congregational polity.

*4.* The Mennonite understanding of *ethics* is based on discipleship with a strong concern for simplicity in lifestyle, honesty and peace, the maintenance of group integrity, and minimal participation in and responsibility for the larger society. Until recently Mennonite ethics were shaped significantly by Mennonites' strategic withdrawal from the wider society.

*5.* The fifth distinctive is Mennonite ambivalence toward *mission.* In contrast to Anabaptists who understood their raison d'être to be mission, Mennonites have been preoccupied with conservation. The mindset and ethos of historical Mennonitism has been nonmissionary. The Anabaptists were dynamically missionary. By comparison the ethos of modern Mennonites is conventional Protestant. Protestants (whose origins lay in the reformation of church structures and doctrines) and Roman Catholics face no such contradiction. Christendom was nonmissionary in outlook and both Protestants and Roman Catholics worked to keep the Christendom framework intact. For Catholics and Protestants alike mission became the vocation of missionary orders and voluntary groups rather than the concern of the church qua church.

Mennonite missions have been oriented more to duty and obedience by the select few than to spontaneous witness of the whole church.

The thrust of the foregoing analysis is that at critical points there is fundamental discontinuity between historical Anabaptism and its lineal descendent, Mennonitism. This is particularly true with regard to a theology of mission, as the next section seeks to show.

CONTRIBUTORS TO A THEOLOGY OF MISSION FOR MENNONITES

A number of important background influences have contributed to the development of a Mennonite theology of mission.

*Nineteenth-Century Spiritual Awakening*

One of the significant influences is the spiritual quickening of Mennonites in the nineteenth century. This quickening owes a great deal to the Pietist movement, especially in Germany and Russia, and to recurring waves of revival in North America. One of the early mission promoters among American Mennonites was Samuel Haury, already mentioned in chapter 2.[1] Haury received missionary training at the Rhenish Missionary Training School at Barmen, 1871–75, an influential Pietist institution, and then offered himself for missionary service on his return from Germany. The General Conference Mennonite Church appointed him to work among the Arapaho in 1880.

Mennonites were also influenced deeply by the revival message and methods that were rapidly introduced across the western world in the nineteenth century. At the same time Mennonites began to feel the impulses set in motion by the wider Protestant missionary movement. The modern missionary movement dates from the beginning of the nineteenth century and grew in strength throughout this period. The movement itself was both a product of and a stimulus to renewal. With its appeal to the biblical injunction to "Go into all the world" at a time when new means of transportation were making the whole world more accessible, this powerful initiative drew Mennonites along.

---

[1] Samuel S. Haury, *Letters Concerning the Spread of the Gospel in the Heathen World Presented to All Mennonites in North America,* trans. Marie Regier Janzen and Hilda Voth (Scottdale, Pa.: Herald Press, 1981); originally published as *Briefe über die Ausbreitung des Evangeliums in der Heidenwelt* (Halstead, Kans., 1877).

In summary, the nineteenth century proved to be a crucial period for Mennonites.[2] During this time several centuries of cultural isolation began to break down. Mennonites increasingly were exposed to the wider Christian church. At the end of this century the basic institutional framework for future church life was established, including mission agencies, publishing houses, educational institutions at the secondary and higher levels, and conference structures. All of this was accompanied by an accelerated acculturation to North American society, particularly in the twentieth century.

## One Hundred Fifty Years of Missionary Experience

The century and a half of missionary experience that Mennonites have had since the nineteenth century awakening has shaped the sending church in ways never anticipated. This experience has irreversibly altered Mennonite horizons. This impact has occurred on both domestic and foreign fronts. Domestically, this has meant a new engagement with the urban world as well as with other ethnic groups. Although the bulk of Mennonite congregations remain in rural areas, they have been deeply influenced by urbanization and industrialization. By definition mission involves crossing cultural and political boundaries. The experience of encountering diverse cultures around the world has internationalized the Mennonite horizon, especially since World War 2.

Three learnings can be gleaned from these years of cross-cultural experience. First, from a *historical* perspective, we have gained a new appreciation of the fact that all cultures and institutions are relative. No culture may be regarded as the standard by which to judge other cultures. Second, we have learned that every *theological* expression is time-bound, each one shaped by a particular context or tradition. Consequently, each theological statement must be understood as partial and incomplete. Third, from a *sociological* point of view, we have discovered the importance of context. Along with others who participated in the modern missionary movement, Mennonites have moved from a concern for indigenization to a concern for

---

[2] For brief overviews, see Theron F. Schlabach, *Gospel Versus Gospel: Mission and the Mennonite Church* (Scottdale, Pa.: Herald Press, 1980), chap. 1; and James C. Juhnke, "Prologue," in *A People of Mission: A History of General Conference Mennonite Overseas Missions* (Newton, Kans.: Faith and Life Press, 1979), 1–14.

contextualization. It is increasingly clear that the proper posture for the missionary is not that of answer-giver but fellow-learner.

## Modern Missionary Movement

Mennonites have also learned much from the modern missionary movement. Mennonites have been ecumenical borrowers. Participation in this missionary movement has itself become the occasion for increased contact with and cooperation in various ventures. In some instances Mennonites have sought out these associations to meet their own needs for fellowship and camaraderie. More significantly, during the first century of Mennonite missions, from 1870–1970, they relied almost wholly on the ideology and missiology of the missionary mainstream. Mennonites were not writing theologies of mission or manuals on missionary methods during the greater part of this century.[3] This meant that Mennonite missionaries largely accepted the guidelines set by the Protestant mission movement in matters of methodology and rationale.

Indeed, Mennonites owe a great debt for what they have appropriated from the wider movement. They have depended to a great extent on the literature produced by missionary councils and agencies. Perhaps most important of all was the impact made by the Student Volunteer Movement on college-age Mennonite youth in the first decades of the twentieth century.

## A Vision

Since the mid-1940s the Mennonite imagination has been stirred by a vision, the Anabaptist vision as first articulated by Harold S. Bender in 1944. As the movement to recover the Anabaptist vision gained momentum, it was increasingly evident that Anabaptism posed a challenge—perhaps "threat" would be more accurate—to historical Mennonitism in regard to mission. The work of Mennonite missions has produced a double effect. The formation of new Mennonite bodies in various parts of the world has resulted in the spread of Mennonites throughout the world, but this raised unsettling questions about the content of their identity. What remains unclear is the extent to which that identity can be clarified and shaped by Anabaptist perspectives.

---

[3] Cf. "Bibliography of Mennonite Missions," *Mission Focus* 12 (December 1984). This comprehensive bibliography of writings by Mennonites on missions up to 1984 reveals no significant consideration of mission theology or the biblical basis of missions prior to 1940.

At the end of the twentieth century Mennonitism was suffering an identity crisis. At least three streams of influence have contributed to this sense of crisis. The first is the so-called ethnic Mennonites who continue to have a confused identity in relation to the wider culture. They are increasingly accommodated to that culture but not without a guilty conscience. The second stream consists of other ethnic groups that have been joining this Mennonite reality over the past decades. Gradually they have discovered they cannot fully integrate into traditional Mennonite culture. They are attempting to appropriate those elements of a theological and ecclesiological vision of Christian discipleship that attracted them in the first place. But this same gospel-inspired vision has also spurred them to reclaim their own cultural and historical past. The third group that is participating in this crisis are the new Mennonites in Asia, Africa, and Latin America. They too are asking who they are theologically, historically, and culturally. Recovery of the Anabaptist vision may well rest with people outside North America and Europe less inhibited by social location and institutional security.

## Renewal

Another contributor to a theology of mission for Mennonites is found in the movements of biblical theology and Holy Spirit renewal, including the so-called charismatic movement, which has affected many of those directly associated with Mennonite missions over the past generation.

## Need for a Theological Foundation

Finally, the felt need for an articulated theological foundation for Mennonite mission propels us forward. The various theologies of mission available from mainstream Protestants, evangelical Protestants, Roman Catholics, Orthodox, and Pentecostals all contribute valuable insights. But none of these can speak out of the historical Mennonite experience. People directly involved in mission recognize the gap between theological vision and ideal, on the one hand, and what happens in practice in the field. This disjunction is underscored by the fact that there are now two and three generations of Mennonites in some churches in Asia, Africa, and Latin America who themselves look and feel more like evangelicals or Protestants than Mennonites. What is the significance, then, of Mennonite identity at all? It is evident that Mennonite missionaries frequently placed low value on their Mennonite heritage as they went about their work, and that they had little clarity about what it might mean missiologically. Thus the outcome is not surprising. And yet Mennonites in the nonwestern churches are asking for help in understanding Mennonite identity in order to be able to decide whether they want to grow in that direction or remain what they are.

The need for a clear theological identity takes on even greater urgency when we recognize that the Mennonite churches in the nonwestern world all live as minorities, and frequently in hostile environments. They want to be prepared to stand in the times of testing that continue to be their lot, and at a time when western Mennonitism is more clearly identifying with the mainstream of the western social, economic, and political realities.

Therefore, the challenge to articulate a foundation for a theology of mission for Mennonites is an important opportunity to clarify Mennonite identity—to move beyond maintenance and self-preservation to mission. The quest for recovery of the Anabaptist vision, which never realized its promise in the historical heartland of Europe and North America, lies in this direction. It will not be found in building more museums, holding more folk festivals, visiting more historical sites, and tracing more family genealogies. To recapture the Anabaptist vision we must above all else embrace a missionary consciousness.

TOWARD A MENNONITE THEOLOGY OF MISSION

As demonstrated above, a theology of mission in the Mennonite tradition will be the product of a variety of influences. Such a theology of mission will seek to draw on the core theological ideas that have been passed down from the Anabaptists of the sixteenth century and that have shaped the Mennonite movement, but it is the task of theology to refocus the whole in light of the *missio Dei*. A Mennonite theology of mission must reflect the drive for a holistic theology that holds in tension proclamation and demonstration of the gospel, evangelization and reconciliation, preaching peace and making peace, advocating for justice and working for justice. Anything less than this will lead to a reduction of the gospel to a fragment of the whole.

*Introduction*

In 1984 an attempt at a comprehensive bibliography of Mennonite missions was published in *Mission Focus*.[4] This bibliography carried some 865 items, beginning with the pioneer Dutch Mennonite missionary to Indonesia, Pieter Jansz, writing in 1859 on the problems of Dutch

---

[4] "Bibliography of Mennonite Missions," *Mission Focus* 12 (December 1984).

colonial policy. This bibliography excluded articles that appeared in the official denominational organs, plus the long list of items in the *Bibliography of J. D. Graber's Printed Writings with Index*, compiled by Steven D. Reschley and Barbara Nelson and published separately in 1980. Graber was the most prolific Mennonite writer on mission themes prior to 1965. Of the items included in this "Bibliography of Mennonite Missions," less than five percent, or approximately forty, have been classified as dealing with the theology of mission.

For purposes of this study we shall exclude the J. D. Graber writings. He saw his role to be that of educating his constituency by drawing on the best missiological insights coming from the wider missionary movement, rather than of attempting to work out an explicitly Mennonite approach to these questions.[5] By the same token, we will also exclude the considerable body of writings by G. W. Peters, the Mennonite Brethren professor of missions at Dallas Theological Seminary who self-consciously wrote as an evangelical for evangelicals.[6]

Although the mission theme did not figure prominently in the early phases of the "recovery of Anabaptism" movement, already in 1946 Franklin H. Littell made the case for interpreting sixteenth-century Anabaptism as essentially a missionary movement.[7] He developed this

---

[5] An exception to this generalization is his contribution to the H. S. Bender Festschrift. See J. D. Graber, "Anabaptism Expressed in Missions and Social Service," in *The Recovery of the Anabaptist Vision,* ed. Guy F. Hershberger (Scottdale, Pa.: Herald Press, 1957), 152–66.

[6] See J. B. Toews, "George W. Peters: A Measure of the Man," in *Reflection and Projection: Missiology at the Threshold of 2001,* ed. Hans Kasdorf and Klaus W. Müller (Bad Liebenzell: Verlag der Liebenzeller Mission, 1988), 26: "He did not see the Mennonite Brethren Churches as only a segment of the larger Mennonite-Anabaptist but a distinct entity with a theology of its own which was neither particularly Mennonite nor Anabaptist. He saw the future of the Mennonite Brethren Church in the mainstream of Evangelical Christianity of America. The concern for world mission as the passion of his life at times seemed to overshadow his deep commitment to a basic Anabaptist understanding of theology." This Festschrift in honor of G. W. Peters (1908–1988) includes a bibliography of his writings.

[7] In conversation David A. Shank has reported being present when Littell first presented his paper in 1946 with Harold S. Bender in the audience. Bender acknowledged that in formulating his "Anabaptist vision" statement three years earlier he had overlooked the centrality of mission to the Anabaptist movement. In Bender's *These Are My People: The Nature of the Church and Its Discipleship According to the New Testament* (Scottdale, Pa.: Herald Press,

thesis fully in *The Anabaptist View of the Church: An Introduction to Sectarian Protestantism*.[8] This was followed by two doctoral dissertations in German and one in English: Wolfgang Schäufele, *Das missionarische Bewußtsein und Wirken der Täufer* (1966);[9] Georg Gottfried Gerner, *Der Gebrauch der Heiligen Schrift in der oberdeutschen Täuferbewegung* (1973);[10] and Ray C. Gingerich, *The Mission Impulse of Early Swiss and South German–Austrian Anabaptism* (1980).[11] The last in particular focused the importance of missionary consciousness for Anabaptist identity. Each of these studies reinforced the historical picture of sixteenth-century Anabaptism as a movement seeking to live out the Great Commission in its day as the apostolic vanguard. But throughout the period 1945–1970 no one undertook to work out a theology of mission for today from an explicitly Anabaptist/Mennonite perspective.

In 1967 Mennonite Brethren scholars produced a Festschrift, *The Church in Mission*,[12] in honor of longtime missions and educational leader J. B. Toews. This volume contained a section on "Historical Recovery of Mission," which included chapters on sixteenth-century Anabaptists and the Pietists of the seventeenth century.

Hans Kasdorf's thorough study of Mennonite Brethren mission thought for the period 1885–1984 yields several observations and conclusions that are applicable to Mennonites more generally. The Mennonite Brethren have largely depended on others for the mission language they have used. And this borrowed language has, in turn, reshaped them in the direction of "American Evangelicalism and

---

1962), chapter 5, he attempts, rather obliquely, to include mission in his discussion of ministry.

[8] Franklin Hamlin Littell, *The Anabaptist View of the Church: An Introduction to Sectarian Protestantism* ([Hartford?]: American Society of Church History, 1952). Republished as *The Origins of Sectarian Protestantism: A Study of the Anabaptist View of the Church* (New York: Macmillan, 1964).

[9] Wolfgang Schäufele, *Das missionarische Bewußtsein und Wirken der Täufer* (Neukirchen-Vluyn: Neukirchener Verlag, 1966).

[10] Georg Gottfried Gerner, *Der Gebrauch der Heiligen Schrift in der oberdeutschen Täuferbewegung* (Thesis, University of Heidelberg, 1973).

[11] Ray C. Gingerich, *The Mission Impulse of Early Swiss and South German–Austrian Anabaptists* (Ph.D. diss., Vanderbilt University, 1980).

[12] A. J. Klassen, ed., *The Church in Mission* (Hillsboro, Kans.: Mennonite Brethren Publishing House, 1967).

Fundamentalism—more than Mennonitism."[13] Kasdorf summarizes the development of a theology of mission among Mennonite Brethren in several stages: implicit holistic theology; salvationist theology emphasizing the love of God and the cross of Christ; kingdom theology—incarnation as model, church as instrument of kingdom, spiritual gifts bestowed for ministry by the whole people, all members are called to be servants of the King; a trinitarian theology. These stages, of course, overlap and intertwine, but in each stage a particular theme was dominant. Kasdorf concludes that a theology of mission is always in process of development. What is needed is an overarching vision of the direction in which this development ought to take us.[14]

With the decade of the 1970s we began to see self-conscious efforts to develop a theology of mission within the Mennonite tradition. A flurry of articles appeared around 1975, and several collections of essays have appeared since that time. In 1983 Donald R. Jacobs published *A Pilgrimage in Mission,* with the avowed purpose

> to study what part modern missions have played in increasing and decreasing these tensions within the brotherhood; to propose a way of understanding missions whose foundation is scriptural; and to reflect on some of the lessons God has taught us Anabaptist Mennonites who have been preserved and nurtured for over 450 years by God.... It is only in participating with God in his mission that the Anabaptist people and, for that matter, any denomination, find fulfillment. So this study is not only a study of the church's mission but of the church itself.... For Mennonites, hopefully this book can help update our understanding of how we can maintain both a vision for a 'pure church' and a vision for a 'missionary church.'[15]

It remains to be noted that the most significant theological influence during the period 1955–1980 was that of John Howard Yoder. His seminal work, *The Politics of Jesus,* was published in 1972 and, together with his many other writings, was deeply formative for subsequent missiological developments.[16] Yoder both clarified the continuing

---

[13] Hans Kasdorf, *A Century of Mennonite Brethren Mission Thinking, 1885–1984* (Th.D. thesis, University of South Africa, 1986), 332–33.

[14] Hans Kasdorf, "Toward a Mennonite Brethren Theology of Mission," *Mission Focus* 16 (March 1988): 1–6.

[15] Donald R. Jacobs, *Pilgrimage in Mission* (Scottdale, Pa.: Herald Press, 1983), 14, 19.

[16] John Howard Yoder, *The Politics of Jesus* (Grand Rapids: Eerdmans, 1972).

missionary significance of the believers church vision and criticized the lack of integrity in Mennonite church life.[17]

*Basic Sources Used*

The method adopted here has been to select certain texts, largely published in the journal *Mission Focus* during the years 1973–1980, that have contributed to the development of a missiology growing out of the Anabaptist/Mennonite theological vision. These include pieces by David A. Shank, "The Shape of Mission Strategy,"[18] "Anabaptists and Mission,"[19] "Towards an Understanding of Christian Conversion,"[20] and "The Shape of Mission";[21] Wilbert R. Shenk, "The Dynamics of Mission";[22] Robert L. Ramseyer, "The Anabaptist Vision and Our World Mission (I)";[23] Takashi Yamada, "The Anabaptist Vision and Our World Mission (II)";[24] Marlin E. Miller, "The Gospel of Peace";[25] John Driver,

---

[17] See Yoder's various contributions to *Concern: A Pamphlet Series for Questions of Christian Renewal,* nos. 1–18 (1954–1971).

[18] David A. Shank, "The Shape of Mission Strategy," *Mission Focus* 1, no. 3 (January 1973): 1–7; reprinted in *Mission Focus: Current Issues,* ed. Wilbert R. Shenk (Scottdale, Pa.: Herald Press, 1980), 118–28.

[19] David A. Shank, "Anabaptists and Mission," in *Anabaptism and Mission,* ed. Wilbert R. Shenk (Scottdale, Pa.: Herald Press, 1984), 202–28.

[20] David A. Shank, "Towards an Understanding of Christian Conversion," *Mission Focus* 5, no. 2 (November 1976): 1–7.

[21] David A. Shank, "The Shape of Mission," *Mission Focus* 8 (December 1980): 69–74.

[22] Wilbert R. Shenk, "The Dynamics of Mission," *Mission Focus* 1, no. 2 (November 1972): 1–3.

[23] Robert L. Ramseyer, "The Anabaptist Vision and Our World Mission (I)," *Mission Focus* 4, no. 4 (March 1976): 1–6. Reprinted in *Anabaptism and Mission,* ed. Wilbert R. Shenk (Scottdale, Pa.: Herald Press, 1984), 178–87.

[24] Takashi Yamada, "The Anabaptist Vision and Our World Mission (II)," *Mission Focus* 4, no. 4 (March 1976): 7–14. Reprinted in *Anabaptism and Mission,* ed. Wilbert R. Shenk (Scottdale, Pa.: Herald Press, 1984), 188–201.

[25] Marlin E. Miller, "The Gospel of Peace," *Mission Focus* 6, no. 1 (September 1977): 1–5. Reprinted in *Theology for the Church: Writings by Marlin E. Miller,* ed. Richard A. Kauffman and Gayle Gerber Koontz (Elkhart, Ind.: Institute of Mennonite Studies, 1997), 3–12; also reprinted in *Mission and the Peace Witness: The Gospel and Christian Discipleship,* ed. Robert L. Ramseyer (Scottdale, Pa.: Herald Press, 1979), 9–23.

"Mission—From a Believers Church Perspective";[26] Mennonite Board of Missions, "A Theology of Mission in Outline";[27] and Hans Kasdorf, "Toward a Mennonite Brethren Theology of Mission."[28] Although not incorporated in this study, two volumes have been published more recently that bring together subsequent work: *Anabaptism and Mission*[29] and *The Transfiguration of Mission*,[30] both edited by Wilbert R. Shenk. Finally, a compendium of papers originating from a consultation sponsored by the Council of International Ministries, titled *A Relevant Anabaptist Missiology for the 1990s*,[31] will repay careful study.

*Defining Themes*

Ten main themes run through these writings; these themes will be examined in turn.

*1. Mission originates in God's mission to redeem the world.* The specific missions in which we engage are responses to the *missio Dei.* This statement is the fruit of a long development in missiological thought. From the beginning of the modern mission movement the basis of mission was established by identifying the motive. Over time various motives have been advocated.[32] What we observe is that the motivation

---

[26] John Driver, "Mission—From a Believers Church Perspective," *Mission Focus* 7, no. 1 (March 1979): 1–6. See also John Driver, "A Missionary Community," chap. 6 in *Community and Commitment* (Scottdale, Pa.: Herald Press, 1976).

[27] The Mennonite Board of Missions, "A Theology of Mission in Outline," *Mission Focus* 6, no. 5 (May 1978): 9–13; also printed as a pamphlet by MBM.

[28] Hans Kasdorf, "Toward a Mennonite Brethren Theology of Mission," *Mission Focus* 16 (March 1988): 1–6.

[29] Wilbert R. Shenk, ed., *Anabaptism and Mission* (Scottdale, Pa.: Herald Press, 1984).

[30] Wilbert R. Shenk, ed., *The Transfiguration of Mission* (Scottdale, Pa.: Herald Press, 1993).

[31] Calvin E. Shenk, ed., *A Relevant Anabaptist Missiology for the 1990s* (Elkhart, Ind.: Council of International Ministries, 1990).

[32] R. Pierce Beaver, "Missionary Motivation through Three Centuries," in *Reinterpretation in American Church History,* ed. Jerald C. Brauer (Chicago: University of Chicago Press, 1968), 113–51; Johannes van den Berg, *Constrained by Jesus' Love: An Inquiry into the Motives of the Missionary Awakening in Great Britain in the Period between 1698 and 1815* (Kampen: J. H. Kok, 1956); J. A. de Jong, *As Waters Cover the Sea: Millennial Expectations in the Rise of Anglo-American Missions, 1640–1810* (Kampen: J. H. Kok, 1970).

for mission has been fluid. Historical perspective and context have been of critical significance in shaping understandings of mission in particular eras. The sociopolitical forces have had great influence on the motives for mission in successive periods. It is clear that we cannot rely on motives for mission to provide us with a sure basis for Christian mission.

A new concept emerged after 1950. Gerald H. Anderson studied representative writers for the period 1928–1958 and demonstrated the continuing profusion of ideas concerning the basis of mission. Anderson identified six different positions, including culture-centered (A. G. Baker), human-centered (Vernon White), church-centered (Roman Catholic), Bible-centered (Harold Lindsell), kingdom-centered (E. Stanley Jones), Christ-centered (John A. Mackay). Nevertheless, Anderson discerned an emerging trend toward a theocentric/trinitarian basis for mission. In the early 1950s the concept of *missio Dei* was introduced and has gained wide acceptance.[33]

Mennonites played no direct role in these debates about the starting point and motives for mission, but their engagement in missionary work since 1850 exposed them to the range of missiological issues. They have readily embraced the emerging theocentric position. The biblical theology movement also exerted a salutary influence with its emphasis on Jesus Christ as Savior and Lord, the foundation for mission and ethics.

If we read the Scriptures from the standpoint of God's missionary intention, at least three points stand out. First, the basis of that salvific plan is *agape* (John 3:16–17; Rom. 5:8; 1 John 4:7–21). It is God who takes the initiative in seeking out humankind. God does this not because men and women deserve to be delivered from the power of sin but because that is in the nature of *agape*. Second, God's ultimate purpose is "to unite all things in Christ," that is, to liberate men and women from the power of death, their mortal enemy. This salvation redounds "to the praise of his glorious grace" (Eph. 1; Col. 1:15–29; Rom. 8:20–23; Rev. 4:11–5:14, 7:9–12; Ezek. 36:16–32; Isa. 43:1–44:8). Third, the Bible shows God acting in a threefold manner. We meet God first of all as loving creator of the world and humankind. Next we encounter God as redeemer, the one who patiently and in grace continues to seek out a people who respond to God's love. Finally, the Bible discloses God as the consummator, the one who guarantees the outcome of history and

---

[33] Gerald H. Anderson, *The Theology of Missions: 1928–1958* (Ann Arbor, Mich.: University Microfilms, 1960), 343.

leads in the triumph of good over evil. God is shown to be a missionary God: the one who initiates, comes to the world seeking and wooing, calling and restoring. By contrast, all human efforts to work out salvation are futile.

2. *Mission is essentially a messianic movement led by the Suffering Servant in the power of the Spirit.* God's missionary intention for the world is entrusted to the Messiah, the one called Suffering Servant. A major theme in Old Testament prophecy is that the people of God will finally find rest, that is, salvation, when the Messiah comes. This prophecy concerning the Messiah reaches a high point in Isaiah. The prophet Isaiah envisaged the day when God would do a new thing in human affairs through the Messiah. The Old Testament contains three strands. One strand has to do with the Messiah, "the anointed one," the just and righteous king who will reign in the future. The second strand is Daniel's prophecy concerning the Son of Man. The third strand is Isaiah's vision of the Suffering Servant.

Jesus fuses these three strands by embodying all three within himself. The coming of Jesus inaugurates a movement. Peter's sermon at Pentecost reaches its climax with the recognition of Jesus as the Messiah (Greek: Christ) when he asserts: "Let all the house of Israel therefore know assuredly that God has made him both Lord and Christ, this Jesus whom you crucified" (Acts 2:36). From the New Testament record it is evident that Jesus was deeply conscious of his call to carry out God's plan from the moment of his baptism by John the Baptist. Jesus' public ministry is a working out of that obedience. Jesus became the Suffering Servant of God by whom the world was reconciled to God. Jesus was aware that as Son of Man he was elected to inaugurate God's new order. This is evident in the way Jesus initiates his ministry. He begins with this announcement: "Repent, for the kingdom of heaven is at hand" (Matt. 4:17; cf. Matt. 4:23, Mark 1:14, Luke 4:18–21).

Early in his public ministry eyewitnesses sensed the extraordinary character of Jesus. Matthew notes: "And when Jesus finished these things the crowds were astonished at his teaching, for he taught them as one who had authority, and not as their scribes" (7:28–29). Instinctively the disciples interpreted this special character through conceptual categories from Judaism such as "eschatological prophet" or "political Messiah-king." But such categories did not correspond to Jesus' self-awareness. Only gradually, and after much struggle and confusion, did the disciples eventually break through to new insight.

Following the death, resurrection, and ascension of the Lord, the community of disciples was gripped by the conviction that God had entrusted the whole outcome of history to the One, the Suffering Servant whom they now acclaimed Lord and Christ. The presence of the Holy Spirit further attested to the messiahship of Jesus. Integral to messianic expectations was the promise that the Spirit of God would be fully present in the Messiah. The life and witness of Jesus gave convincing evidence that he was truly Spirit-anointed. Ultimately, he would claim that "all power is given to me," thus linking himself with God in the power of the Spirit.

We should recall that this christological development in early Christianity occurred in the context of missionary engagement. The surrounding cultures and religions regularly and vigorously challenged the Christian witness. Caesar presented himself as *kyrios* and Christians had to stand against this idolatry or be co-opted by it. Thus, the early Christian witnesses were cast in a role of confrontation with opposing forces of various kinds—religious, traditional, political, and social.

Mission may also be viewed as messianic movement from the sociohistorical angle. In the 1960s two notable works appeared: *A Theology of Hope* (1967) by Jürgen Moltmann, and *A Rumor of Angels* (1969) by Peter Berger.[34] As a theologian, Moltmann drew attention to the importance of hope for understanding human experience. This eschatological dynamic propels history forward. Sociologist Berger's book serves as a complement to Moltmann's. Berger's purpose was to challenge the conventional wisdom regarding secularization. He identified five "signals of transcendence" that attest to the enduring reality of religion even in so-called secularized societies. One of these signals is the universal and irrepressible human need for hope.

In *The Sociology of Hope*, Henri Desroche studies messianism and millenarianism sociologically and historically.[35] He documents the pervasive role this dynamic has played in human experience. Desroche analyzes the messianic/millennial dynamic as it moves through a

---

[34] Jürgen Moltmann, *A Theology of Hope: On the Ground and the Implications of Christian Eschatology* (London: SCM Press, 1967); Peter L. Berger, *A Rumor of Angels: Modern Society and the Rediscovery of the Supernatural* (Garden City, N. Y.: Doubleday, 1969).

[35] Henri Desroche, *The Sociology of Hope* (London: Routledge and Kegan Paul, 1979); originally published as *Sociologie de l'espérance* (Paris: Calmann-Lévy, 1973).

succession of three stages: from oppression to resistance to liberation. Drawing on the insights of Desroche and theologian John H. Yoder, David Shank summarizes the processes and stages in the outworking of the messianic dynamic.[36]

 *a.* In the midst of oppression, domination, and injustice, someone appears as God's instrument for bringing about a new humanity— interpreted as new creation, new kingdom, new order—visualized as a holistic reality encompassing religious, social, economic, and political aspects of life.

 *b.* Those who break with the old order to follow this messianic leader form a new community that becomes a critique of the old order and a foreshadowing of the new when it is achieved fully.

 *c.* When the promised ideal new humanity fails to appear, the initial impetus wanes and the movement undergoes a fission, one part veering in a religious direction and the other taking on political forms. The breakup thus diffuses and denatures the original holistic thrust. Each wing becomes in itself a movement that reinterprets the original holistic intent, but from a reductionist perspective. (Veering toward the religious means abandoning the political, and vice versa. Yet the vision of the messianic kingdom holds the whole together.) This reductionist stage may continue for a long time.

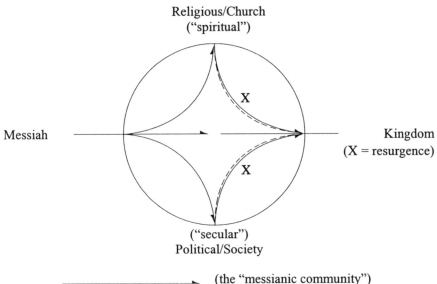

---

[36] David A. Shank, "The Shape of Mission," 72–73.

*d.* But with the passage of time and the emergence of new conditions and demands, the inadequacies of the present order become apparent. This ferment and growing dissatisfaction form the seedbed for a messianic resurgence. A new leader arises who interprets once again the possibility of a holistic new order. This resurgence moves toward the messianic core message and draws on the vision and dynamic.

*e.* Desroche suggests that early Christianity understood itself as a millennial/messianic movement.[37] With the rise of Augustinian theology in the fourth and fifth centuries, millenarian consciousness waned. The church had now moved from being in the position of an oppressed minority to being in a dominant role in society. Desroche concludes, "Thus messianism is a plan for a Kingdom conceived in the lands of Exile."[38] The bane of the people of God has been that they frequently forget that they have been liberated from exile and allow themselves to be seduced by the old enslaving order once again.

*3. The missionary's task is to announce and witness to the Messiah's reign.* As we examine the witness of the early church, we note that it had two focal points. On the one hand, the first Christians understood that they were to continue the works characteristic of the kingdom that Jesus had inaugurated but which were yet incomplete. In giving the Great Commission, Jesus establishes the structure for this ongoing ministry through the community.

The goal of mission then is the fulfillment of the Messiah's reign. This goal becomes the touchstone for determining and evaluating missionary action. What is authentic will be faithful to this messianic vision, and what is false and contradictory will be opposed to the messianic goal. As missionary experience shows, our obedience is always less than perfect and consistent. Therefore we need constantly to keep before us a standard by which to guide and correct our undertakings.

The history of missions demonstrates that as the Scriptures are released into new churches—although imperfectly and unfaithfully transmitted—the originality and power of the message can break through again and the messianic core will stimulate fresh movements. Ultimately, every attempt to channel, control, and institutionalize the messianic

---

[37] Cf. the bold use made of this paradigm by John G. Gager, *Kingdom and Community: The Social World of Early Christianity* (Englewood Cliffs, N. J.: Prentice-Hall, 1975), chap. 2.

[38] Desroche, *Sociology of Hope,* 112.

dynamic is doomed. Humanly speaking, we can only respond to and follow after the Messiah; we cannot put ourselves in charge and determine the exact course the movement must take.

   4.  *The Messiah's message is the gospel of peace.*[39] The New Testament writers employ a variety of terms to describe the gospel: good news of the kingdom; gospel of God/gospel of Jesus Christ; gospel of salvation; and gospel of peace (Acts 10:36; Eph. 2:13–22). All of these terms refer to the same reality. In Jesus the Messiah, God has made possible our redemption from sin. This results in a new relationship with God (at-one-ment) and with other men and women. As members of this reconciled community we are called to live out the messianic peace and actively invite others to accept the offer of God's shalom. The messianic order is characterized by the commitment to peace. Jesus Christ consistently rejected the use of violence in effecting God's reign through him in the world. This is paradigmatic for the messianic community.

   5.  *Mission strategy grows out of the nature of this messianic movement.* Some of the most tragic chapters in the history of the Christian movement have been written when zealous people have resorted to methods and strategies that fundamentally contradicted the messiahship of Jesus. Whenever violence and subterfuge have been the hallmarks of witness, the results have been counterproductive. We must always strive for integrity between the messianic community's life and its witness. This is the ultimate test of regeneration and new birth into the life of the messianic kingdom. To put the matter positively, in the Sermon on the Mount, Jesus described his community as light and salt. This means that the essential values of the new order are to characterize the life of the community.

   Vicarious sacrificial suffering is also integral to missionary witness.[40] Against the backdrop of his own public ministry, death, and resurrection, Jesus addresses the disciples: "As the Father has sent me,

---

[39] Cf. Marlin E. Miller, "The Gospel of Peace"; and John Driver, "A Community of Peace," chap. 5 in *Community and Commitment* (Scottdale, Pa.: Herald Press, 1976).

[40] Two studies that link atonement and mission demonstrate how theology is enriched when it is grounded in mission: John Driver, *Understanding the Atonement for the Mission of the Church* (Scottdale, Pa.: Herald Press, 1986); and C. Norman Kraus, *Jesus Christ Our Lord: Christology from a Disciple's Perspective* (Scottdale, Pa.: Herald Press, 1987). Both books were written in missionary contexts.

even so I send you" (John 20:21). Thus, the Messiah's example and model is made normative for the community. Jesus modeled servanthood, and transformed lordship into servanthood (Mark 10:45; Isa. 53:10–12). This statement is not first a doctrine of the atonement but rather a description of a missionary lifestyle (cf. Phil. 2:5–11). According to the Apostle Paul, voluntary renunciation of our own program in favor of the Messiah's is at the heart of missionary obedience (cf. 1 Cor. 1:17–2:5).

6. *The goal of mission is the establishment of the new order under the Messiah's rule.* That is, mission is the means by which God is establishing the reign of God in the world. In the first place, this means that mission leads to the formation of concrete communities living out the new order which Jesus inaugurated. In other words, the messianic movement must be rooted in specific times, places, and among particular peoples. But there is also the universal/cosmic thrust. The Apostle Paul asserts that it is God's intention to unite all things in Jesus Christ. We must hold together the particular and the universal. Typically, the particular becomes the path to the universal.

Reflecting on the mission task, we make several observations. First, the world belongs to Christ by right of creation and redemption. But in this age, the world remains in the grip of the evil one. Second, God sent Jesus to liberate the whole of creation from the power of evil. Third, the basic dynamic in history is this conflict between Christ and anti-Christ, between the forces of good and evil. Fourth, the missionary witness is addressed into that conflict where the battle rages. We do not understand Christ or our salvation apart from meeting Christ at work in the world redeeming the world. Finally, the outcome of this struggle has already been decided. Jesus Christ can already be acclaimed victor, and those who place their faith in Jesus and live in fellowship with him are assured of a share in that victory.

7. *The church is both the first fruit of this messianic movement in the world and the primary carrier and instrument of messianic purpose.* As such, the very nature of the church is missionary. The church's vocation is prefigured in the calling of the people of God beginning with Abraham in Genesis 12:1–3: "By you all the families of the earth shall bless themselves." The phrasing of this promise emphasizes several things. First, it is universal in scope: "all the families of the earth." Second, it emphasizes the instrumentality or vocation of the people of God rather than according them a privileged status. Third, it strongly suggests a servant relationship. The people of God are available; through

you the peoples "shall bless themselves." God acts through the community. Isaiah describes the vocation of the people as that of being a "light to the nations" (42:6–7). God also views the church as collaborator. In the words of the Apostle Paul, "that through the church the manifold wisdom of God might now be made known to the principalities and powers" (Eph. 3:10). And the church is the means through which God's power is being displayed before the world (3:20–21).

The Bible describes no other means by which God is reaching out to the world than through the people of God.[41] Through this people the witness becomes concrete and incarnate. This people actualizes God's love.

*8. Mission is an act of radical obedience and discipleship.* The sixteenth-century Anabaptists were noted for their frequent reference to the Great Commission.[42] They correctly sensed this commission to be definitive. For the Great Commission provides a permanent structure for the church in its relationship to the world. God loves the world and Jesus Christ died for the world, thus making possible the forgiveness of sin and opening up a new future. This is at the heart of the apostolic proclamation which Jesus commissions his disciples to carry to all parts of the world (Matt. 28:16–20, Mark 16:15–18, Luke 24:46–49, John 20:19–23, Acts 1:6–8).

Being converted to Jesus Christ begins with the fundamental decision to *turn* Christ-ward, but it includes embracing the mission of Jesus to the world. The disciples are in the world but not of the world; and the disciples are sent into the world as the apostolic vanguard for the salvation of the world. Whenever the church turns its back on this commission, it loses its identity and authority, and surrenders its integrity.

---

[41] Cf. Wilbert R. Shenk, "The Great Commission," in *Mission Focus: Current Issues* (Scottdale, Pa.: Herald Press, 1980), 41–46, for a brief study of the varying emphases of the five versions of the Great Commission. These enrich and enlarge the scope of Christ's command. The biblical vision of the church as God's missionary agent is explored richly in John Driver, *Images of the Church in Mission* (Scottdale, Pa.: Herald Press, 1997). We need to reclaim this biblical foundation.

[42] Franklin H. Littell, "The Great Commission," chap. 4 in *The Origins of Sectarian Protestantism: A Study of the Anabaptist View of the Church* (New York: Macmillan, 1964).

This missionary witness is, of course, perceived by the world as judgment on it. The Gospel according to John puts the matter pointedly: "This is the judgment, that the light has come into the world, and men loved darkness rather than light, because their deeds were evil" (John 3:19; cf. 12:30–32). To be faithful in witness requires that we maintain a clear perspective on the radical nature of the missionary call and the crucial role mission plays in the outcome of history.

*9. Mission requires deep penetration into the world—for the world, against the world.* Missionary obedience involves penetration into all areas of life, for all of life is to be brought under the lordship of Jesus Christ. The gospel is as comprehensive as the new order that it announces. The power and persuasiveness of the gospel is precisely that it alone offers an adequate alternative to the old order that is in the grip of the forces of death and destruction. This of course demands a deep respect for and understanding of culture, social and economic structures, and political reality, in order that we may truly communicate good news in those precincts. The vision of the new order suggests the scope of the task—the breadth, depth, and priorities that arise out of the gospel.

The Incarnation is basic to all missionary approaches. God chose Incarnation, complete identification, as the means by which to reach the world through the Messiah. What God did in the Incarnation of Jesus the Messiah was, of course, unique and cannot be repeated. But Jesus challenged his disciples to follow him into the world as he had been in the world, identifying with humankind in order to witness to God's new order of salvation. The Incarnation judges all missionary methods by calling into question those that reduce the gospel to fit the missionary's categories or that truncate the gospel in order to squeeze it into our preconceived notions, methods, and strategies.

*10. The present age is the missionary age, the age of the Holy Spirit, the time between Pentecost and Parousia.* Pentecost marks the inauguration of this age; Parousia will signal its ending. The Holy Spirit mediated to the church the power of the resurrection and confirmed to the church that Jesus Christ was indeed the ascended and exalted Lord. The Holy Spirit released into the body the power and grace of Jesus the Messiah. The work of the Spirit is to extend the Messiah's reign. Jesus Christ has never relinquished his claim to the whole of creation. Yet parts of that creation are living in rebellion and the Messiah's sovereignty is not acknowledged everywhere. But the sovereignty of the Messiah will indeed be made manifest when "his enemies become his footstool" (the Old Testament phrase most quoted in the New). The state, for example, is God-ordained to maintain order in human society, but the state does not in fact submit to Jesus Christ as sovereign. Even the church frequently fails to honor Christ's rule fully.

Nonetheless, through the community of the Spirit, Christ's authority and saving presence is being extended in the world. The formation of the people of God in every part of the world is basic to the realization of God's plan, for this people are the vanguard of the new age.

This present time is marked by the tension of the "already/not yet." This is the age in which the Messiah's people live in anticipation of the consummation of their salvation. They live amid the continual struggle between Christ and antichrist. Although they are confident that victory is assured, the battle is not yet over. This is the age of ongoing struggle between Christ and Satan, between the old and the new orders. This is the age of the martyr and of redemptive suffering. But this is also the age when, through the fulfillment of the Great Commission, Christ's plan to redeem the world will be completed. Then Jesus the Messiah will be acclaimed as King of kings and Lord of lords (1 Tim. 6:13–15; Rev. 19:13–16).